The Life of Stuff

Simon Shaw Donald was born in La
was educated at Garrion Academy
University. He became a profession
mainly in new plays at the Traverse 1
also in television and film. His credits   ...for include the
stage plays *A Tenant for Edgar Mortez*, *In Descent* and *Prickly Heat*; television dramas *Deacon Broadie*, *The Ebb-Tide*, *The Last Frontier*, *Low Winter Sun* and *Methuselah*; feature films *The Life of Stuff*, *My Life So Far*, *Beautiful Creatures*, *Sleep Without Dreams* and *Thylacine*. He is married to the photographer Carol Gordon and they live in Edinburgh.

Capercaillie Books

The Life of
Stuff

by Simon Donald

Capercaillie Books

CAPERCAILLIE BOOKS LIMITED

Published by Capercaillie Books Limited,

Registered Office 48 North Castle Street, Edinburgh.

First published by Theatre Scotland in 1992 © 1992 Simon Donald.

Revised version published in anthology *Made in Scotland* by Methuen Drama in 1995 © 1995 Simon Donald.

The moral right of the author has been asserted.

Design by Ian Kirkwood Design.

Printed in Great Britain by Antony Rowe Ltd., Chippenham, Wiltshire

Set in Cosmos and Veljovic

A catalogue record for this book is available from the British Library
ISBN 0-9545206-6-1

The Publisher acknowledges support from the Scottish Arts Council towards the publication of this title.

The Life of Stuff was first performed at the Traverse Theatre on 1st August 1992.

For Carol

Introduction

The play was originally commissioned by Max Stafford Clark at the Royal Court Theatre in London. At that time I was working regularly as an actor at the Traverse Theatre in Edinburgh. Iain Brown, artistic director at the Traverse, read the first draft and thought it would make an appropriate piece to open the new building, as the Traverse was about to move from the old Grassmarket to its present, custom-built building next to the Lyceum. We both liked the idea of a group of characters rattling around in a strange environment – much as the actors were in the new Traverse building.

The first draft had no gags. Iain Brown thought this was a big mistake and so from the first draft on, *The Life of Stuff* gradually mutated into a comedy.

The whole play stemmed from an initial image of a miserable little guy, shivering in his underpants in a cellar, shaving his head with a Bic razor over a washing-up bowl. All round him a world of violence and madness, drugs and demented dreams.

The play is full of lunatic imagery – Ancient Egypt, Outer Space, burning men and boa constrictors – simply because the characters' heads are full of this stuff – dreams of escape and exoticism, power and influence, drugs and sex. The language is largely unpremeditated – in this night-time pressure cooker where no-one leaves and everybody gets madder and madder, the characters speak the thoughts in their heads without cencsorship.

In every production I've been involved with there's been an important moment where the actors realise that the play works best when you grasp this idea, that the characters speak their thoughts, unfiltered, unpremeditated, unprepared.

I was very deeply immersed in the first production – rewriting as the actors rehearsed – having great fun with stuff that came up in the rehearsals. Stuart McQuarrie, who has played Leonard three times now – in the first production, the second production at the Donmar Warehouse and in the very rarely seen movie version – gave me my favourite gag. I'd written that Leonard, the inadequate psychopath, was plagued by eczema, a condition which continually undermined his status as a convincing heavy. Stuart revealed that he also had been plagued by eczema and was also an inadequate psychopath (though that was my own insight based on observation) and when we talked, and I asked him what was the worst thing about having eczema, he told me that what drove him nuts was the fact that in Scotland everybody always referred to it as 'ig-zeema'. This actually annoyed him more than the itch. It became a defining characteristic about Leonard. That not being listened to, not being understood, not being heard – ig-zeema not – eczema troubled him more than life and death or the awful ig-zeema itch.

It was astonishing watching the second production of the play. I suppose in the very first production of a new play, you agonise so much about whether or not the most basic things work – is that funny? is that moving? is that interesting? – that you can fail to see how much fun might be had once the basics have been taken care of. At the Donmar Warehouse, under the direction of Matthew Warchus, the piece just took off into the stratosphere. I watched it and had that weird 'man, did I write this' feeling.

And Matthew achieved this magnificent energy – what he did was, instead of having scene changes, he would have all the lights black out at the end of a scene and as the new scene was arranged, in the darkness around the last character to speak from the previous scene, he'd sustain a single, slowly narrowing focus-spot on their shocked or startled face, and that would be the main focus on the stage, until the next scene was in place around him. (I still picture Dougie Henshall's startled puss, frozen in the spotlight's glare, sweat beading, lip quivering, eyes darting unreliably.) Then when the focus had pulled in to a close-up on his face, the focus-spot blanked out and the rest of the stage banged into lit life and action. The effect was very much like a movie cut and it so sustained the energy of the play. It was thrilling.

The play also has a soundtrack — what Leonard's playing at the beginning is by definition whatever would currently most annoy someone of Arbogast's generation. We found in both the original productions that Frank Sinatra (from the swamp of Arbogast's subconscious) provided amazingly useful and com-plementary scene change/transition cues. Especially a song called 'How Little We Know' — which, spookily, summed up the whole play. (A song which, despite my long and abiding love of Frank Sinatra, I'd never heard till we went on a trawl through his entire ouvre.)

So it made sense to play it at the interval — as though Big Frank was on hand to make sense of the whole ghastly experience.

Simon Donald, 2004

Characters

ARBOGAST

HOLLY

EVELYN

LEONARD

DOBIE

JANICE

FRASER

SNEDDON

Prologue

Blisters nightclub.

This is the dark and intimate interior of Alec Sneddon's nightclub Blisters. Alec Sneddon takes the mike to say a few words to his friends. He's at a mike-stand on the nightclub stage, surrounded by sparkly lights and tons of cigarette smoke. He has a boa constrictor draped around his neck.

SNEDDON: Mister Willie Dobie walks right in here. With his 'Proposition'. I says to him – Fuck off, Willie Dobie – that is not a 'Proposition', that's a joke. He's a joke. Willie – you are a joke . . . He has the gall. The unmitigated gall – comes into my club with his demands! And what? I roll over and play dead? What say I remove those few brains you have in your skull – Buster! Shove them up your bottom keep your small intestine company, eh William? Extract your spinal column. My old china. Proposal my arse. You people are children, Willie. I am laughing in William Dobie's face. You want to get into bed with me? It's many, many light years beyond your bedtime . . .

SNEDDON is on the stage. Delilah the boa constrictor is draped round him. SNEDDON holds Delilah's head so that he can speak into her eyes. They look at each other up close.

SNEDDON: Let you come between me and my baby, eh Delilah?. . . **(His voice is a loving, teasing whisper.)** Oh sure thing, Mister 'So Called William Dobie Esquire'. **(His friends have gone quiet.)** Aye – in your dreams, pal.

SNEDDON tenderly kisses the snake.

Scene 1   Mutiny

Very loud club music. Late afternoon. Main party space in the warehouse. A stack of cleaning implements, buckets, mops, some shovels and rubbish bags with bits of rubbish hanging out. In the room are JANICE, who is slumped somewhere asleep, EVELYN, HOLLY and LEONARD. The girls are all in various versions of their best party clothes. A professional disco sound system is set up on a raised platform.   LEONARD is playing with it. The volume crashes up and down, the music stops and starts. The lift arrives, the lift doors open and ARBOGAST bounces in, a sweeping brush in either hand.

ARBOGAST: Righty ho! Arses in gear! People! I've to tell you there's work to be done. Turn down that din son. No – turn that racket off, Leonard.

EVELYN: He says he's got to get balanced.

ARBOGAST: Am I speaking to you, doll?

EVELYN: Evelyn.

ARBOGAST: I said there is work to be done. We've this floor to get swept for starters, eh? 'Fore somebody cuts themselves. **(To HOLLY, who is dancing)** And that includes you as well, doll.

HOLLY: Did he say work?

EVELYN: He did.

ARBOGAST: Yup, that is what he said. **(To LEONARD)** Turn that . . . Hey. Leonard. LEONARD! I AM KEEPING MY TEMPER HERE!

HOLLY: What work?

LEONARD: Eh? I'm just getting a balance set, Mr Arbogast.

6

ARBOGAST: Turn it off!

HOLLY: I thought it was meant to be a party.

EVELYN: Holly, it's only just gone four.

LEONARD: But I need to set a balance for the party.

ARBOGAST: The party's not till later. Now – we've got jobs to get done. And you do NOT want to get me DEMENTED.

EVELYN: Is there going to be drugs?

LEONARD: I thought this was my job for the party.

HOLLY: Bound to be millions.

ARBOGAST: Playing yourself is not a job, Leonard.

HOLLY: Cause I'm meant to be long term unemployed. And this is supposed to be a party. So what's with all this talk about work and no guarantee of any drugs. I mean . . . fucks sake.

EVELYN: I don't think he means that kind of work. Do you?

ARBOGAST: What are you pair on about?

HOLLY: I mean I have actually been told I'm UNEMPLOYABLE. Never mind just unemployed.

EVELYN: When did you get told that?

HOLLY: I've actually got it officially down on my records.

ARBOGAST: This is not that kind of . . . Look! **(To LEONARD)** I am TELLING YOU FOR THE LAST TIME NOW!

HOLLY: Not just on the one record either. So I take what he's saying quite personally.

EVELYN roars at LEONARD.

EVELYN: Hoi! Can you can that racket for ten seconds, Scabby!

7

LEONARD turns the music off.

LEONARD: This is beyond belief. Willie said I was in charge of . . .

ARBOGAST: LEONARD!

LEONARD: I am supposed to be . . .

ARBOGAST: LEONARD!

LEONARD: Look, it's up to me to . . .

LEONARD finally realises he's getting up everybody's noses.

LEONARD: All I'm trying to do is get it all set up right so that when it comes to the party everybody can have a nice time, that's all – no need to all get in such a . . .

ARBOGAST has gone to LEONARD and put his arm around him.

ARBOGAST: People having a nice time is none of your concern, Leonard. Tell you what, son. **(He dangles a set of car keys in front of LEONARD'S nose.)** Willie wants you to fetch up some champers out his Merc for him. Eh?

EVELYN: And give us all some peace.

LEONARD: And who's that tart calling 'Scabby'?

ARBOGAST: Probably you, Leonard.

LEONARD: Cause it's eczema.

He takes the car keys.

ARBOGAST: Probably because of your pronounced eczema.

LEONARD: It's not pronounced ig-zeema, it's pronounced eczema.

ARBOGAST: This place has got to get cleared up.

LEONARD: Well what about them?

ARBOGAST: They'll help.

EVELYN: Long as we don't have to touch.

ARBOGAST: Now that is a wee bit uncalled for, doll.

HOLLY: Nervous eczema isn't contagious. Just repulsive.

EVELYN: Any sort of rash makes me nervous. Stop calling me doll you.

HOLLY: Anyway I'll bet you can get drugs for it.

EVELYN: Bet you can't at this party.

LEONARD: Do this pair think they're being amusing, cause they're about as funny as frintic systosis.

ARBOGAST finally loses his temper.

ARBOGAST: This is NOT a PARTY! The PARTY is NOT till LATER! Do you all UNDERSTAND!

HOLLY: Well what has Dobie made us get all dolled up for then?

LEONARD: That's 'dolled up'?

ARBOGAST: Will you be QUIET!

EVELYN: **(to LEONARD)** See, now you've got him demented.

ARBOGAST: And behave like fucking ADULTS! I have to raise my bloody VOICE all the time.

HOLLY: Whoah here a minute. Now I think that that is a perfectly reasonable question. Why we were told by Willie Dobie to get as dolled up as possible because he was asking us — personally In-Viting us to be his own personal guests at the party of a lifetime.

9

EVELYN: With drugs.

ARBOGAST: Because when the party starts you chicks are floozy. And before the party starts you two chicks are CLEANERS. And . . . (**indicating JANICE**) bloody wake her up as well, Leonard.

LEONARD goes to wake JANICE up. He shakes her gently, mumbling to her quietly, as though he's fond of her. The lift arrives with WILLIE DOBIE in it.

ARBOGAST: And, I might add, you do not get to become floozy until you have acquitted yourselves as bloody cleaners.

EVELYN: So who says we're interested in being bloody 'floozy'?

ARBOGAST: Cleaners don't get drugs.

DOBIE: And THAT, if I may say so, is where you and I part company, Davey. Personally I'd be loath to describe any one of the three young ladies present as 'floozy'.

ARBOGAST: I know it requires a bit of a stretch of the . . .

DOBIE: And I mean that in a purely constructive sense. (**To JANICE**) Welcome to the land of the living, petal. I have to say you look radiant after your wee siesta.

JANICE throws up on the floor. A big, splurgy, alcoholic-poisoning, stomach emptier.

JANICE: Fuck. Missed my frock.

Everybody stares at her. She straightens her squinty wig.

JANICE: Thank God, eh? Party still going? (**To LEONARD**) Get your mits off me ya scabby pervert!

EVELYN: (**to HOLLY**) Aw, right. So THAT'S floozy!

JANICE: Any drink? I'm totally parched . . . (**She clocks

DOBIE.) Have you got my rent book sorted yet?

DOBIE: Davey, why don't you see if you can find the young lady a drink for her upset tummy and we'll get her details re-organised in due course. I mean, you know . . . Party Time!

ARBOGAST: Sure thing, Willie, anything you say, sir. **(He pulls her up by the arm.)** 'Mon you.

JANICE clutches a polythene bag and her own handbag. ARBOGAST leads her to the lift. Over his shoulder to HOLLY and EVELYN:

ARBOGAST: You'll need a bucket and a mop as well, you pair.

DOBIE: Ha ha. Some man, Arbogast.

The lift leaves.

DOBIE: A phenomenon. **(To LEONARD)** Get a bucket and get that seen to like you've been told . . . eh . . .

LEONARD: Leonard.

DOBIE: I know that. Leonard.

LEONARD: Straight away, Willie.

He gets a bucket and mop.

DOBIE: **(to the girls)** Phenomenal guy, Davey Arbogast. A bona fide self-made man. Totally. Self-made. Mind you, that probably explains why he's such a mis-shapen fucker. Haha. Dragged himself up from the gutter that boy did. Got himself educated at the College of Hard Knocks. The University of Life. Mind you, he never graduated because he missed all his tutorials and the neighbour's dog ate his notes. Eh? **(He puts his hand in his inside pocket.)** Either of you chicks feel like helpin me do some drugs?

11

Scene 2   Disguise

The basement of the warehouse. FRASER, in his underpants, shaves his head over a basin. A small tranny on the floor plays music. The lift arrives and the doors open. ARBOGAST and JANICE get out. FRASER looks up.

FRASER: Aw come on you, this isnae fair. You said you were going to bring me some clothes, fucks sake. And a towel.

ARBOGAST: You've just to ignore him, doll.

FRASER: Aye, join the club.

JANICE: **(to ARBOGAST)** That's it with the 'doll' you. Okay. Enough. **(Looking round the basement)** You promised me there was drink down here. **(To FRASER)** I've just flung up and I'm totally dehydrated. **(To ARBOGAST)** I've met him before . . . **(to FRASER)** haven't I? **(To ARBOGAST)** This is him that was waiting in my room, isn't it? That you sent me up to give the van keys to, isn't he?

FRASER: So? **(To ARBOGAST)** What the fucks she doin here anyway?

JANICE: So? **(To ARBOGAST)** What does he mean 'So?' So I'm just tryin to be civil and . . . confirm . . . that we've met. **(To FRASER)** That's 'So'. **(To ARBOGAST)** So how's he got no clothes on and what's he doin to his head?

FRASER: He's burnin my clothes as evidence. **(To ARBOGAST)** Right?

ARBOGAST: Sure thing, Fraser.

JANICE: Eh?

FRASER: So that I don't get connected to the insurance number. **(To ARBOGAST)** Right?

ARBOGAST: That's right enough, son.

JANICE: **(at the haircut)**. And that's your disguise, is it?

FRASER: Oh, very good.

JANICE: You better grow a beard as well when you've shaved your nut.

FRASER: Oh I had, had I?

JANICE: Uhuh you better. Cept then you'd look the same as you did before except your head'd be on upside down. **(Cackles)** Sorry Fraser. **(More cackles as she looks at him standing there with his Bic razor and his half-shaved head)** No really, sorry. **(Pause)** God, are you no frozen Fraser . . .? **(Mild paroxysm)**

FRASER: Ay, I am.

JANICE: **(through drunken giggles)** . . . Freezin Frozer?

FRASER: **(to ARBOGAST)** What is this?

JANICE: Hoi . . . **(They look at her.)** Careful you don't nick your scalp . . .

ARBOGAST: She's pished, that's what.

JANICE: . . . with your razor Fraser . . .

FRASER: I can see she's pished. I can SMELL she's fuckin pished. Look at her. That's no what I mean. I mean what's she doin here. I thought I was supposed to be in hiding till you lot gave me my plane tickets for me and Raymond. How can I be in hiding if you bring stupid pished women in? I mean what if she identifies me. That's hardly in hiding, is it? Do you lot not know what in hiding is? Or am I supposed to do an insurance number on her as well. Eh?

ARBOGAST: She's brought some clothes for you, **(to JANICE)** havent you? **(JANICE still hasn't recovered.)** Eh Janice?

(She looks at him.) Clothes?

JANICE: Oh right. Clothes. **(She hands the poly bag to ARBOGAST.)**

FRASER: And a towel?

ARBOGAST: She hasn't got a towel. **(He empties the clothes on the floor next to FRASER and gives him the poly bag.)** Use that.

FRASER rubs his head with the poly bag then starts to separate the clothes. ARBOGAST looks at the pile of clothes and picks out a pair of lime green y-fronts.

ARBOGAST: These are redundant are they? Unless you want to swap.

He sticks the underpants in his pocket.

JANICE: Nobody told me about a towel. Just clothes. For a man. **(Pause)** But I didn't have any. **(She lights up a cigarette.)**.So I went into Leonard's room. He's the room next to me. Snores like a drain. Dirty washing all over his floor. **(FRASER is putting on a pair of luridly odd socks.)** And I couldn't put the light on cause me and Leonard don't get on and he'd be all over me if he woke up and saw me in his room at night going through his dirty washin on my hands and knees cause he's a sex-starved pig and no wonder . . .

FRASER is putting on a jumper.

FRASER: For fucks sake I can't wear this on a beach – it's scratchy nylon.

JANICE: So I definitely didn't want to wake him up.

ARBOGAST: It'll keep you warm the now.

JANICE: Cause he's a light sleeper.

FRASER is putting on the trousers.

FRASER: And these are greasy.

JANICE: Cause he's got weeping sores.

FRASER: Cryin out loud.

JANICE: As a result of his horrific eczema.

ARBOGAST: **(to FRASER)** Quit moanin you.

FRASER: **(to JANICE)** Whose eczema?

JANICE: Leonard's.

FRASER: Leonard who?

JANICE: Leonard scratchy-nylon-jumper-Leonard!

FRASER: Oh, no! **(Pulling the jumper over his head.)** I'm no wearin this!

JANICE: Sticky socks Leonard.

ARBOGAST: **(to JANICE)** Shut up you. Fraser – it's fuckin NERVOUS eczema, he canny help it.

JANICE: **(snorts)** Help it if he wasn't so nervous about washin.

FRASER: **(pulling the socks off)** Are the trousers his as well?

JANICE: Yup. **(To ARBOGAST)** You never said they had to get cleaned.

ARBOGAST: **(to JANICE)** Shut it. **(To FRASER)** Fraser . . .

FRASER: Right! **(He starts to take the trousers off. To JANICE)** Scuse me but I canny wear these.

JANICE: I don't care. **(To ARBOGAST)** But he doesnae ever do a laundry.

ARBOGAST: Keep them on, Fraser son.

JANICE: **(to ARBOGAST)** Or lift the toilet seat either.

FRASER: Bugger off you!

He sits, kicking the trousers off his legs.

ARBOGAST: Fraser son. **(Goes to him)** Calm down a bit.

FRASER: Will you fuck off will you.

ARBOGAST pinches FRASER'S nipple and wrings it hard. FRASER yelps and convulses. Everybody freezes.

ARBOGAST: Fraser listen to me son. I have to tell you to calm down. **(Pause. FRASER recovers. ARBOGAST does it again. Then he puts his hand on FRASER'S shoulder.)** You've to behave yourself and no be difficult or you'll just end up in more bother. **(He takes the cigarette from JANICE and sticks it in FRASER'S mouth.)** Calm your nerves and pull yourself together and Willie'll get round to you and the doll after he's finished gettin things set up for the big party. Okay. Okay? **(FRASER stands, the cigarette dangling from his lips, nervous.)** Okay!?

FRASER: Aye, sure. That's okay then.

JANICE: That's my last cigarette. And we'll have less of the doll you!

ARBOGAST turns to face JANICE. He reaches out and does to her nipple exactly what he did to FRASER'S. JANICE reacts in exactly the same way FRASER did.

ARBOGAST: I've to tell you to behave yourself as well, doll. **(A beat, then FRASER laughs.)**

FRASER: Bet that's sobered you up, eh Janice. Nothin like a

good tweak round the nipples to bring us all to our best behaviour. **(Laughs)** Well . . . fuck me, I think I've really got the eczema in proportion now. See if you see Leonard will you tell him from me that Fraser says thanks for the clothes and we all hope your weeping sore bits get better soon.

ARBOGAST: I'll pass that on. Anything else?

FRASER: Yes there is. Where's Willie Dobie and my tickets he promised me for Ibiza?

JANICE: And my rent book?

ARBOGAST: Everything's all goin to get taken care of for the both of you in the fullness of time. We're busy bees just now so don't be pests.

He gets in the lift and leaves.

FRASER: **(holding out the cigarette)** Here.

JANICE: What?

FRASER: I don't smoke.

JANICE: Oh. I've got another packet anyway. I wish I was you and I could just have battered him.

FRASER: I know I should've. Who the fuck is he anyway? Hurting people.

JANICE: He's Willie Dobie's people hurter. So what stopped you then?

FRASER: Because I don't have any clothes on, do I. And you can't batter som'b'day in your underpants. And there's no way I'm putting any of that stuff on again ever.

Scene 3   Big Plans

WILLIE DOBIE, EVELYN and HOLLY on the roof. WILLIE is expansive, showing off and fantasising. He opens a bottle of champagne and has a swig. EVELYN is about to put some drugs up her nose. The exact identity of the powder in use is never fully ascertained. HOLLY and WILLIE have already had some and are both sniffling. EVELYN is staying well away from the edge of the roof.

DOBIE: First time I saw this place and looked at this view . . . I recognised my own dream. Whoof! What do you see? Eh?

HOLLY: Well it's quite a long way down, isn't it . . .

DOBIE: Every individual a dot. And every dot a customer.

HOLLY: I mean you wouldn't be a dot, you'd be a splotch.

EVELYN: Holly don't . . .

DOBIE: A Heaving Metropolis of desperate dots!

EVELYN: . . . do you mind if I don't look cause I'm not personally very good at heights.

DOBIE: A Swirling Galaxy of Bottomless Opportunities!

HOLLY: **(to EVELYN)** Look up then! **(Big sniff)** God. My nose is all lovely and numb.

DOBIE: Potential?. . . Fuckin Astronomical!

EVELYN: **(hesitating before she snorts)** Is this the stuff that makes you randy or the stuff that makes you think you can fly?

HOLLY: Randy.

EVELYN: I hope so cause I'm dreadful at heights.

HOLLY: Or fly. Can't really tell yet.

EVELYN: **(lightly sniffs the powder to identify it)** Better no be or I'm off. Either way. Smells to me a wee bit like Shake 'n'Vac. **(To HOLLY)** Did that stuff he gave you smell like Shake'n'Vac?

HOLLY: Nup.

DOBIE: Just get it up your face and take a look at this view.

EVELYN snorts. They wait. She lifts her head up to look at the view and then drops it immediately, spluttering.

EVELYN: Fucks sake I can't see ANYTHING. What is this? Clean-o-Pine.

DOBIE: No it is not Clean-o-Pine and it is not Shake'n'Vac and nor is it One Thousand and One Dry Bloody Foam either. It's . . . it's . . . **(sniffs)** It's supposed to be top quality recreational chemicals. Mind you, it just goes to show you never could trust that swine Alec Sneddon.

EVELYN: Aw God, you never bought this off Mad Alec Sneddon did you. Fucks sake. **(She tries to snuffle the stuff out of her nose.)**

DOBIE: No you're right there, darling, I did not 'BUY IT' off of Mad Alec 'Psycho Nutter' Sneddon.

EVELYN: Cause he's responsible for a significant amount of local brain damage. Ask her.

HOLLY: Any local brain damage I've got you've got as well, Evelyn. All you ever do is moan, you, anyway. It's a waste of drugs givin you drugs. Cause you don't know how to enjoy yourself.

EVELYN: Holly, people who don't like heights don't enjoy being up on roofs looking at views.

DOBIE: Well his brain damaging days have only just very

recently ceased. Anyway, it'll no do you any harm. Keep you nice and perky till the other stuff gets here. Have a slug of this to get rid of the taste.

He passes her the champagne. She has a swill at it.

HOLLY: Well I think it's a gorgeous view. I could just stand here and . . . in the breeze . . . it's giving me goose bumps and . . . you know what it feels like when somebody breathes on the back of your neck and then blows in your ear and you open your eyes and you're in a steamy jungle and it's not a person, its a big throbbing leopard . . . and . . . **(She tosses her hair and shivers.)** . . . could somebody put their arm round me a minute please cause my bottom has gone to jelly. **(DOBIE willingly does so.)**

EVELYN: Oh right. So it's obviously not the stuff makes you think you can fly then. Maybe if you stayed away from the edge your arse might firm up a trifle.

DOBIE: **(over his shoulder to EVELYN)** A jelly trifle, eh? Haha.

EVELYN: **(miserably, to herself)** What a tube.

HOLLY: What is it that your dream's about?

DOBIE: **(starting to warm to HOLLY)** My dream?

HOLLY: Yes. The view in your dream. I mean what's the vision in your view? Apart from . . . lots of buildings. I mean, I can see it's a view of all those buildings, I just felt that you . . .

DOBIE: That I what?

HOLLY: Well that you . . . You know. Were describing the view more sort of . . . I don't know . . . 'symbolically'.

DOBIE: **(to EVELYN)** Hear that? My my, that's awful . . .

EVELYN: Tubeish?

DOBIE: No not tubeish, you – perceptive. Give us that here. **(He swipes the champagne back and gives it to HOLLY.)** No, you're quite right. It's a metaphorical view of a vision.

HOLLY: In your dream?

DOBIE: Uhuh. No. Not in my dream, I mean forget the dream for a minute, I'm talking about real life here at the moment cause I'm not just some half-arsed fucker that has dreams. This is about reality that I'm saying. Tough, hard, down-to-earth circumstances. I've bought this building. And that's a concrete reality. I mean it's one thing having a dream and it's another thing to open a nightclub in a prime site with a captive market and eliminate your competition.

EVELYN: You pair have had different drugs from I have.

DOBIE: **(to HOLLY)** I'm standing on an investment. And I'm looking at the future.

HOLLY: Me?

DOBIE: No, no you, the view. Well. Maybe you as well, I don't know. I mean I'm involved in the property game AND the people game . . . but at the moment I'm only referring to the property version . . .

HOLLY: Although you might want to invest a stake in the right person sometime in the future.

EVELYN: Holly, he's given us different chemicals.

DOBIE: . . . yeah . . .

EVELYN: Cause I can see the Social Security Benefit Office from up here . . .

DOBIE: Eh?

EVELYN: Behind the Magistrates' Courts . . .

HOLLY: So you can.

EVELYN: Next to the Police Station.

DOBIE: Is that what that is?

EVELYN: Yeah. Opposite the Scottish Communist Party Headquarters.

DOBIE: Aye, okay, forget the fuckin view then. What I'm referring to is about what we're standing on. **(Both girls look at their feet.)**

HOLLY: Which is what. Exactly?

DOBIE: Quite literally, a veritable Gold Mine!

EVELYN: Symbolically?

DOBIE: Of course symbolically, are you stupid.

EVELYN: Hoi. Just because we haven't got a job and we live in one of your flats and we pay you an excessive fortune in rent which, thank fuck we get off the council, doesn't necessarily mean I'm stupid, excuse me.

HOLLY: **(pokes him in the chest)** Or! . . . That we're sex slaves! Frankly.

DOBIE: Eh?

EVELYN: Or. Literally!

DOBIE: **(A pause. Then a big hug round each girl's shoulder, pulling them to him. DOBIE cackles.)** My my, haha. It's great to see that a lifetime's dead-end disappointment and unemployability hasn't dented your senses of humour.

HOLLY: I know. I didn't mean to offend you with that thing about sex slaves.

EVELYN: Eh?

HOLLY: It's just the drugs I took talking.

EVELYN: Hoi, I was offended as well you.

DOBIE: No offence taken . . .

HOLLY: Holly.

DOBIE: Holly. And like I said I have a special pharmaceutical phenomenon lined up as a treat for all my people later in the evening once we get into the full swing of things.

EVELYN: I hope it's not more of Alec Sneddon's kitchen-surface scouring-agents.

DOBIE: No it's bloody well not. You.

EVELYN: Well what is it and where'd you get it and it better be good. Cause she promised me you promised us major chemicals.

DOBIE: Where'd I get it? Where? Did I get it?

EVELYN: Yes. If you didn't get it off of mad Alec Sneddon cause he's the only place I know you can get any.

DOBIE: And where do you think Alec Sneddon gets his, smartypants? Do you think it's delivered from outer space wrapped in tinfoil by anonymous aliens? What – is it teams of Belgian scientists testing them on bunnies in a germ-free environment?

HOLLY: Bet it's the aliens.

DOBIE: We make it. I. I have it made.

EVELYN: You?

DOBIE: Yes. No, not me personally, my . . . **(He gestures.)** My people. As of today.

EVELYN: **(snorting)** Your 'people'.

HOLLY: Aliens can be people as well, Evelyn.

EVELYN: Holly . . . aliens are NOT people as well. And neither

23

are you either Holly, so shut up. **(To DOBIE)** You mean your henchmen.

DOBIE: 'Henchmen' . . . Now that's a lovely idea darling, but who has 'henchmen' in this day and age that we live in?

EVELYN: The Mafia.

DOBIE: Well you know, I suppose, in a way . . . I mean even the Mafia must have once had to start somewhere. Locally.

EVELYN: So is that who you get your drugs from.

DOBIE: Darlin . . .

EVELYN: Evelyn.

DOBIE: Evelyn, darlin, if only it were that sinister . . . I mean as usual the facts are so much less . . . Listen. I find some kid who doesn't know his own potential, who's been stuck in a squalid rut, worrying about his pharmacy exams, and his rent's suddenly gone through the roof and his part-time job for Alec Sneddon takes up all his time and only pays him washers and suddenly he's getting terrorised by guys with eczema and stringy ties. So he comes to see me for a bit of assistance in his time of trouble and I said to him, 'Raymond, son' – or whoever – 'working for Willie Dobie full time means a guaranteed weekly income of one and a half per cent gross on all retailed substances and no more trouble with rent arrears and horrible visitors and maybe one day you'll be able to afford your very own secret laboratory on a floating desert island. Inventing pills to cure the flu.'

HOLLY: I could tell you were a people person as well.

ARBOGAST comes up the roof access ladder.

ARBOGAST: Willie, there's a boy in the basement waiting to see you about a pair of tickets to Ibiza.

DOBIE: Davey! Take a look at that view will you.

ARBOGAST: I know Willie, it's a bloody shame but it canny be helped.

Scene 4   Ibiza

JANICE and FRASER in the basement.

JANICE: Your head's all tufty bits and baldy patches.

FRASER: **(brushing his hand through his mangled hairdo)** I know. It's bloody murder this. You got a mirror?

JANICE: Should have. I was in a hurry. **(She gives him a mirror out of her handbag.)**

FRASER: **(examining the damage in the compact mirror)** God. That's really bad, isn't it.

JANICE: Terrible.

FRASER: I know, you're right. God. I can't believe I'm doin this again.

JANICE: Spoil your holidays.

FRASER: I'm no goin any holidays.

JANICE: I thought you were gettin two tickets to Ibiza.

FRASER: It's not for holidays – it's for me and Raymond to start a new life again.

JANICE: In Ibiza? Doin what?

FRASER: Exotic dancing. **(Pause. JANICE falls about.)** Don't laugh. It's big bucks you. **(He stands.)** Hey! What's so funny? **(He looks down at himself. JANICE is helpless.)** Fucks sake, I wouldn't be doin it in my y's. I'd have a costume. So?

25

JANICE: So?

FRASER: So what's so funny? **(She laughs some more.)** At least I'll be making something of myself.

JANICE: So you will.

FRASER: No just pullin lumbers for my landlord.

JANICE: **(stops laughing)** How do you know what I do for Willie Dobie?

FRASER: Cause I know.

JANICE: How?

FRASER: Just by lookin at you.

JANICE: I did ONE favour for him. And it's the last time I do anything for the sleazy creep and as soon as I get my rent book back I'm off. And it was not a lumber either.

FRASER: Huh.

JANICE: So what did you do? Just by lookin at you.

FRASER: I told you my clothes had all to get burnt.

JANICE: Oh sure thing.

FRASER: So's the insurance company couldn't link me . . .

JANICE: Course.

FRASER: With the burned out vehicle that he's gonnae collect a wad of insurance for . . .

JANICE: Uhuh.

FRASER: . . . that I drove away and set on fire for him . . .

JANICE: Well I entertained mad Alec Sneddon for him for a number of consecutive weekends in Blisters nightclub . . .

FRASER: Oh. OOOhh! Enter-Tained.

JANICE: Yes. With wit and charm. And I never lumbered him.

FRASER: Course you didn't, doll.

JANICE: Yes. And I can prove it can't I and dont call me doll . . .

FRASER: . . . Sure thing. And don't you talk to me about that mad swine Alec Sneddon, cause Raymond and me . . .

JANICE: . . . Ask Arbogast. Cause last night when Alec finally runs me home in his van, Arbogast whapped him on the head and dumped him in the back.

FRASER: Cause Raymond and me . . . **(pause)** Whapped him on the head and dumped him in the back!? . . .

JANICE: **(pause)** Uhuh.

FRASER: Of the van?! . . .

JANICE: . . . uhuh . . .

FRASER: The back of the van . . . that I drove away and set on fire?

JANICE: **(Pause. She turns away.)** God I'm parched. Do you think there's a drink in here?

FRASER: **(pause)** Eh. I'll have a wee look in a minute. **(Pause. They reflect.)** You're right, it's quite stuffy in here, isn't it. **(Pause)** Do you think he woke up?

JANICE: I don't . . . It was a fair wallop he got hit.

FRASER: Oh. Good. **(Pause)** What was he like as a person?

Scene 5   Violence

LEONARD and ARBOGAST in the main party space. ARBOGAST is slugging whisky straight from the bottle and smoking a stubby wee cigar. LEONARD is sweeping up and being in the huff.

ARBOGAST: So what's the matter with your puss? **(LEONARD scratches his inner thigh.)**

LEONARD: My ointment's run out.

ARBOGAST: **(double takes, then genuinely pained)** No, Leonard, son I didn't mean that, I meant . . . I meant why have you got such a huffy expression on your face?

LEONARD: I know that's what you meant. Because my ointment's run out. What do you think I thought you meant? It itches like fuck when I exert myself without my cream.

ARBOGAST: Aye, aye, okay son, I'm sure . . . spare me the clinical details. Believe you me I fully sympathise with your dermal plight, Leonard. Tell you what, stick on some Big Frank and join me for a wee snifteroony.

LEONARD: **(very pained)** Do we have to listen to that moanin wop . . . Arbogast? **(ARBOGAST gives him a big look.)**

ARBOGAST: Am I gonnae have to tell you I've to tell you to behave? **(LEONARD puts on some Sinatra, 'The wee small hours of the morning'.)** It's important to relax your soul when you get the chance, Leonard. And you and me are going to be very busy bees in the next few hours.

LEONARD: How can you relax to this?

ARBOGAST: I'll have you know that bit in the Godfather where they garrotte the horse's head is based on this man's vocal style. **(LEONARD joins ARBOGAST. They each have a**

slug of the whisky.) So?

LEONARD: What?

ARBOGAST: How'd it go?

LEONARD: How'd what go?

ARBOGAST: You and the chemist. Give me the details.

LEONARD: Well . . . I gave him the prescription but I didn't have enough cash and I'd forgot my dole card so he said . . .

ARBOGAST: Not THAT fuckin chemist, the wee STUDENT CHEMIST you paid a visit . . .

LEONARD: AWW! . . . wee RAYMOND . . . Aw fabulous, fine! Absolutely fine. Fat wee fuck.

ARBOGAST: **(happy, grinning, ready for the details)** So?

LEONARD: So it's all taken care of and sorted out all hunky dory.

ARBOGAST: Yeah?. . . Come on . . . Don't keep me dangling here on tenterhooks . . .

LEONARD: I just did it like you said. To the letter, you know. As per instructions. **(Modestly sheepish)** Plus . . .

ARBOGAST: Yeh, plus . . .

LEONARD: Plus I added one or two little improvisational extras of my own.

ARBOGAST: Give me a for instance Leonard son? **(LEONARD takes a screwed up polythene bag out of his pocket, uncrumples it and shows the contents to ARBOGAST.)** Is that . . .?

LEONARD: Only a toe. Well he was in his jim jams and I thought he'd need all his fingers for stirring and stuff. Plus! **(He takes a pair of spectacles from his pocket and puts them on.**

29

The specs have scores all over the lenses. LEONARD looks at ARBOGAST.) I checked he had a spare pair first . . .

ARBOGAST: **(not so impressed)** Oh very frightening.

LEONARD: . . . they were in his cagoule though, this is the ones he was wearing!

ARBOGAST: **(still not totally impressed)** At the time?

LEONARD: Aye at the time.

ARBOGAST: Superb Leonard . . .

LEONARD: After I'd chopped his toe off, not as easy as you'd think by the way. I got him on his back and sat on his chest and then switched on my drill and leaned on his lenses.

ARBOGAST: Nice one son, that's a new one on me, Leonard.

LEONARD: Seemed to be a new one on wee Raymond as well.

ARBOGAST: Bloody lucky for the laddy he'd never gone for contacts. And how about the chemicals.

LEONARD: Sneddon's got the boy all fitted out in a lockup garage with the whole kit and caboodle already up and running. I picked Raymond up at the hospital after he'd got his new stump dressed and recovered consciousness and ran him round there. He's gonnae have a load ready for the night.

ARBOGAST: Marvellous. **(He sings along with the song for a line, passing the whisky to LEONARD.)** I'll fetch them myself later. Willie'll be chuffed as fuck.

LEONARD: So . . . should we maybe . . . I mean . . . is Willie expecting . . .

ARBOGAST: What.

LEONARD: It's just that you seem very cool about the prospect of some sudden retaliation from Mad Alec . . .

ARBOGAST: History!

LEONARD: How's that then?

ARBOGAST: **(cackles, up on his feet, enthused, singing)** 'In the wee small hours of the morning' Alec Sneddon finally fucked upwards in a shower of sparks.

LEONARD: How . . . you didn't . . .

ARBOGAST: Leonard. There's minds been at work round here you know. Making sure we have a tidy and viable conclusion in our grasp. I mean at first I offered this one out to tender, two hundred bucks round Willie's flats for any unemployed yo-yo keen enough to do the usual with an iron bar up the close round the back of Blisters when Sneddon closed up on the way home – and are they interested – are they buggery. The spirit of enterprise has fled the lot. See that's a direct result of the sort of campaign of terror that swine has long term waged on the populace. And the fact that they're far too comfy on the fuckin dole. So I had a look at an alternative angle. And Alec Sneddon's history and soot.

LEONARD: What.

ARBOGAST: The baldy boy in the basement. He drove Sneddon's van down to the docks and torched the lot. After Janice had lured him home with her wiles.

LEONARD: I know, she's got fabulous wiles that doll.

ARBOGAST: Leonard. Pay attention to what Old Blue Eyes is telling you. Wiles never phone you back.

LEONARD: So anyway, the baldy boy . . .

ARBOGAST: . . . He thought he was doing an insurance number for Willie. Stupid wee prick. And Alec Sneddon was in the back.

LEONARD: Aw . . . So why did the baldy boy . . .

ARBOGAST: Because, Leonard . . . him and wee fat Raymond are . . . you know . . .

LEONARD: What?

ARBOGAST: . . . You know . . .

LEONARD: What? . . . You mean they're . . .!?*#"

ARBOGAST: . . . Right. So when Fraser finds his . . . his . . . you know . . . "!?*#" . . . has been savagely tortured, with his head kicked in and his toe lopped off and his eyeballs intimidated then Fraser comes to see Willie for help and Willie says do a wee insurance number on the van for me and I'll give you and your . . . your . . . !?*# a set of tickets to go away to Ibiza with and nasty men won't pester you with drills and secateurs anymore.

EVELYN clambers out of a ventilation shaft. She is quite oily and dusty and she has a nosebleed.

EVELYN: They no here?

ARBOGAST: Who's that, doll?

EVELYN: Stop calling . . . Her and Dobie. He was showin us round and chatting us up and suddenly he opens up this hatch and says, on you go, you're first doll, and when I finally find a place I can turn round and crawl back out they've gave me the slip down some dark corridor. And I've been stuck in the ventilation system crawling round on my hands and knees like something out of Alien. And I was fairly sure there was something crawling around behind me cept I thought it was that pair. Or maybe it was just the drugs at last, cept I think the drugs has all bled out in my nosebleed. See when I find him I'm gonnae get some proper drugs off him then I'm gonnae kill him. Cept I'll have to come up with an alternative route into my system instead of up my nose. D'you think he's got that stuff I've heard about you can rub on your gums?

LEONARD: Oil of cloves?

EVELYN: Funny guy. I only turned up because Holly promised me he promised her there'd be sex and drugs. Cept I informed her I wasn't interested in any sex. Just the drugs. I've never had good drugs. I told her I'd come if she PROMISED me he'd promised her good big proper chemicals. Anyway she says she wasn't interested in the sex either and then about the first thing she goes and says to him is by the way we're not your sex slaves, which is the sort of thing she always says to men that give us drugs. So you can see his wee eyes light up and he thinks 'sex slaves – Nice Idea'. And he just ignores the 'we're not' bit. Anyway you can tell by the way she said it that she never meant it anyway. She might as well just have said to him, 'Has the idea of us being your sex slaves ever crossed your mind?' AND he's been telling us crap jokes. Nightmare. If I wasn't so bad at heights I'd have flung myself off the roof. And there's not so much as a sniff of good drugs, just this rubbish that makes both your nostrils haemorrhage simultaneously. Does either of you pair possess such a thing as a clean hanky?

ARBOGAST reaches into his poly bag and pulls out LEONARD'S unrecognisably screwed up underpants.

ARBOGAST: You can borrow this, honey pie.

He gives the underpants to EVELYN who uses them to wipe away the blood from her nosebleed. Then she inspects the stain. She freezes.

LEONARD: Those're my y's!

ARBOGAST: It's alright, the other boy didn't need them.

EVELYN: **(to LEONARD)** Sorry. **(To ARBOGAST)** So is it okay if I keep them then?

Scene 6   Membranes

HOLLY and DOBIE are walking around in the building. He is trying to give her a guided tour but doesn't know his way about all that well.

HOLLY: **(Breathlessly whooping with laughter at what she obviously thinks is the best joke the world has ever heard)** So then . . . then the baby bear turns to the daddy bear and says 'Dad . . .?' and the daddy bear says, 'What, son?' and the baby bear says, 'Dad, what kind of bears actually are we?' And the daddy bear says, 'I'm not quite sure I get your drift, son.' And the wee baby bear says, 'I mean are we koala bears or brown bears or grizzly bears . . . ? And the daddy bear says, 'Well, son, I think we're what's commonly known as polar bears. Why were you asking son?' And the baby bear says . . . he says . . . 'Cause I'm BLOODY FREEZIN!!!'

DOBIE: **(Staring at her while she laughs, clearly not amused)** Very good, hen.

HOLLY: **(nearly helpless, but aware that he's not laughing)** What . . . cause the daddy bear . . . so the wee baby bear . . . cause he thinks . . . so it's just that you don't expect that a bear's gonnae be able to . . .

DOBIE: Aye I know, I get it, it's not that I don't get it, I mean I DO get it. I just don't think it's very funny.

HOLLY: It's a fuck of a lot funnier than that one you told me

34

about the highly successful businessman and the cute wee labrador puppy.

DOBIE: **(Pause. DOBIE looks at her.)** That was not a joke, that was a personal reminiscence.

HOLLY: Oh right. **(Pause)** That's why I didn't get it then, cause I didn't see why it was meant to be funny when he wiped his arse on the puppy . . .

DOBIE: **(taking her arm and moving on)** So pumpkin, here's where we're going to have the . . . the . . . **(He opens a door.)** See, it's heavin with potential this place, you could store coats in that wee room. **(He shuts the door.)**

HOLLY: You could fit in a water bed.

DOBIE: You could . . . you could fit in a waterbed.

HOLLY: You could have one of those machines with straps like Alec Sneddon had. **(She wanders off.)**

DOBIE: You could . . . you could have a machine . . . **(following her)** Hang on a tick there sugar . . . where did you hear about . . .

HOLLY: Cept I think that was for . . . wrapping parcels . . . It was always quite difficult to tell in the dark and some of the substances we had with Alec sort of took up all your attention. His office was brilliant though, I mean I just love the feel of linoleum against your skin. Did you know a boa constrictor is actually dry to the touch?

DOBIE: **(pulling a bag of powder out of his jacket pocket)** Tell you what, rub a fingerful of this on your gums, hen.

HOLLY: On my gums? I've already got no feeling up my nose so I don't know that I fancy numb gums as well right now. What the fuck is it anyway cause it gave Evelyn a terrible nosebleed, where the fuck is Evelyn anyway she's always doing this to me at parties.

DOBIE: Away you go, the party hasn't started. This is the very Champagne of substances from my own personal . . . and I really don't understand why your pal was making such a fuss, cause she was uncommonly privileged to be allowed to suck a quarter of a gramme of this up her face, cause this isn't the sort of thing you fling around willy nilly amongst all and sundry.

HOLLY: She never discovers how to let herself go. **(There is a large trunk in a corner of the room. HOLLY has gradually homed in on it. She opens the lid and reaches inside. She pulls out a jumbled armful of abattoir aprons and wellies and hats. Old and filthy and blood-caked.)** See if you flogged this clobber round the stalls you'd make a mint.

DOBIE: There's every chance that's loaded with mad cow microbes. I'd leave it in the trunk.

HOLLY measures an overall against herself.

DOBIE: I would really. Botulism's torture to shake off.

HOLLY: There's something so attractive about a helpless animal. You know. They're so vulnerable once they've been stunned. Floppy. Do you think it'll be alright if I borrow these? Evelyn'll be green.

DOBIE takes the garment from her and turns her away from the trunk.

DOBIE: Tell you what, poppet. This is the most stunning stuff you've ever had in your proximity.

HOLLY: Cause she's got a real thing about body fluids.

DOBIE: And vulnerable! Hnhh. **(Proffering the packet)** Get a dab of that round your mucous membranes.

HOLLY: I'll have you know I don't possess any mucous membranes for your information. **(DOBIE rubs a dab round his gums. He sticks his finger in the packet and holds his finger out to HOLLY. She eyes it suspiciously.)** I hope you don't think I'm letting you stick that up my nostril.

DOBIE: I'm not interested in your nostril, I'm interested in . . . Open your mouth a minute. **(He prods the finger in her mouth. A pause and then and she clamps her teeth on it. DOBIE yelps.)** What the fuck was that for?

HOLLY: That was for what you did to that poor wee labrador puppy.

Scene 7   Young Lovers

In the basement. The lift doors are open and LEONARD is unloading cardboard boxes. JANICE is slumped, FRASER is restless, pacing about.

LEONARD: What about you pair, huh? Fuckin Terminator 3, eh? I could probably get about five years just for having a conversation with you. D'ye think.

JANICE: No chance.

LEONARD: How no?

JANICE: Cause you're not having a conversation with us, that's how no.

LEONARD: Probably just as well, eh? D'ye no think?

JANICE: Shut up, Leonard.

LEONARD: Oh, hey, sure thing Janice, anything you say. Just don't hit me on the head and tell Arnold here to set me on fire.

FRASER: I see what you mean about him.

LEONARD: **(to FRASER)** Mean about who, you?

FRASER: You, ya tube, that's who.

JANICE: **(to FRASER)** Don't call him names cause he's a pig and he'll batter you.

FRASER: Batter me? I'll batter him, that's who'll batter who.

LEONARD: Fuck me, that is some haircut right enough.

FRASER: You're not kidding there, Leonard.

LEONARD: I know, Arbogast said it was and he's no far wrong.

JANICE: It's his disguise.

FRASER: It is some haircut. Never mind Terminator 3. It's the haircut of a desperate man. Who's either getting his tickets to Ibiza or . . .

LEONARD: Oh, Ibiza eh?

JANICE: He's going to start a new life.

FRASER: Or. It is the haircut . . . of an even more desperate man who's got nothing to lose if he has to stay here cause he doesn't get his tickets to Ibiza. All of a sudden.

JANICE: You said you couldn't batter anyone in your underpants.

FRASER: That was before. I could now. Now that they've seen my new haircut.

LEONARD: Aye well, buster, it'll no be me anybody batters shortly, I'll have you both know, cause when Willie Dobie gets this place done up and running he's making me head of security and the like of you pair'll no even get in in the first place because it'll be definitely no dolies allowed. Only proper public with cash to spare, never mind haircuts and underpants.

FRASER: Tough. I'll be in Ibiza by then anyway.

LEONARD: Mind you I'm no sayin I'll no let you in though, Janice. In that wee number anyway, doll. Willie'll most likely get you a job here anyway, off the books. Cept there's no drinkin while your workin, except I could probably arrange it so we could probably have a staff drink together at the end of the night. Me and you. And then I'll get you up the road. What d'ye say? **(He sits on a box and gingerly scratches his armpits and his crotch and behind his knees.)**

FRASER: Aww! It's all over him, look at that.

LEONARD: Hoi! Ma ointment's run out and see when I work up a sweat. **(He reaches into the box he's sitting on and pulls out a bottle of Taboo.)** So what do you say then, Janice. Me and you. A wee staff drink.

JANICE: Leonard. My head's splittin. I've been in a nightclub all last night using my wit and charm. I've flung up, apparently I've helped get Alec Sneddon, who I quite liked by the way, murdered and I can't stand you. Give it to him, he's staff.

She finds somewhere to crash out. FRASER sits next to LEONARD. LEONARD watches JANICE.

LEONARD: I got it for Janice. She's crazy about theme drinks. Look at her. **(They both look at her.)** The amount of shut eye that doll needs . . . Drives me mad thinking about what she gets up to with that Sneddon animal that makes her that knackered. Her room's the one next to mine, Willie says I can move out you know, but . . . I get in the bath after she's had a bath and the enamel's still warm and sometimes there's wee hairs. But I might as well no exist. She can drink millions and it has no effect on her behaviour whatsoever except when she comes back to the flat I can hear her throw up before she goes to her kip. And I fancy her rotten but no in the way she thinks, you know, no in a caring way, more like just pure . . . complete . . . animal . . .

FRASER: So you're gonnae be the new head of security.

LEONARD: Dead right I am.

FRASER: What about . . . Argoblast?

LEONARD: Arbo-Gast! He moves up.

FRASER: Moves up where?

LEONARD: In Willie Dobie's organisation. Willie goes legitimate and leaves the world of small time crime and criminal dolies behind him and Arbogast becomes his right-hand man and I take over from Arbogast.

FRASER: Doin what?

LEONARD: Whatever's . . . required. You know! I don't know, do I. Whatever Willie Dobie tells us . . . like . . . you gonnae drink that?

FRASER: Nup. Anything else?

LEONARD: **(passes him a bottle of Taboo)** Like . . . and don't you be gettin any big ideas just cause you've murdered somebody . . .

FRASER: . . . don't remind me about . . . I haven't 'murdered' anybody.

LEONARD: Cause there's a lot more to it than that. That's the easy bit.

FRASER: **(not happy with the Taboo)** . . . You got anything in there you can drink? . . . I've got to get something I can drink cause I need a drink. So if murderin somebody's the easy bit what's the difficult bit?

LEONARD: **(finds and passes him a bottle of Mirage)** . . . The violence and the pain. Arbogast says I've got a talent for it. He says I'm like the son he never had. He says I understand discomfort because of my affliction. And it's a job you can do without workin up a sweat which is what I'd like to avoid because that's when my discomfort's at its worst. Especially, Arbogast says, if you approach it psychologically, which is how I'm tryin to think about it when I've time. So if Willie Dobie wants somebody to do something for him, he sends me and Arbogast round to see them and inflict a bit of psychology on them and then he'll offer them protection because anybody who knows Willie knows they can always turn to him for a spot of help when they're in a bit of bother. Especially if it's psychological. **(He grabs FRASER'S arm and twists it behind his back, forcing him face down on one of the palettes. He digs out his poly bag with the toe in it. He inflates the bag like a balloon and rattles the toe around in it.)** Hey, Fraser. Guess what I've got in my bag.

FRASER: What? I dunno.

LEONARD: Do you want a clue?

FRASER: Okay then Leonard, gonnae give me a clue.

LEONARD: **(pause)** It's psychological. **(He shows FRASER the contents of the bag. FRASER looks at it, not knowing what it is.)** Look. That's the first piece of anybody I've ever severed. And now the rest of him works for Willie Dobie all thanks to me.

FRASER: **(suddenly realising it's Raymond's toe)** FU-CKIN HELL! FU-CKIN HELL, MAN!

He stops himself saying any more. The lift arrives and EVELYN gets out.

EVELYN: Is there any bin liners in here, I've got to find some Arbogast says, it's fuckin blackmail this, I'm goin out of my nut on powerful drugs and I've done in my molars with grindin my teeth and he has the gall to tell me I'm no allowed anythin to calm me down till I've helped with the sweepin up. **(During this she finds a roll of bin liners.)** And he also says to tell the guy with the uncomfortable scabs to think about how it's probably about time he tried on the new clobber he's supposed to wear to see if it's an improvement. **(To LEONARD)** I suppose he means you. **(Loudly)** This is HELL! These chemicals are Dangerous! I'm losing my MIND! Oh . . . And I've to tell the other guy with the devastated hairdo he's to stay cool cause he'll get his tickets for Ibiza, whatever the fuck he means by that, your guess is as good as mine buster.

The lift doors close and EVELYN disappears. LEONARD releases FRASER.

LEONARD: Must have got the Shake'n'Vac, it's fuckin lethal. Still whenever wee fat Raymond's finished his chemistry we'll no have to bother with that garbage any more. **(LEONARD looks challengingly at FRASER.)**

FRASER: **(after a pause, innocently)** Wee who . . . ?

LEONARD: Fat wee Raymond McFadyen, the guy that owns the other nine toes. **(He fetches a pair of shoes and a bouncer's D.J. and trousers in polythene.)** Used to work for Alec Sneddon till you burned him. We are talking serious amounts of Substances here. Cause now he works for us! So who is it you're going to Ibiza with, Fraser?

FRASER: Aw . . . Raymond McFadyen the pharmacy student?

LEONARD: Aye. Pal of yours? **(He rips the polythene off the clothes.)**

FRASER: Eh? . . . Not at all, no. He . . . just, he only just moved into the flat a few weeks ago. I mean of course I 'know' him. You can't not 'know' – he's the student. The chubby student. I mean you always get at least one student don't you . . . I fuckin personally hate students, you know?

LEONARD: **(tittering)** I'm tellin you, Fraser, Arbogast's right about this psychological thing, it's fuckin magical. I love it. **(He cackles.)** Hey, Fraser, what do you think of the state of this clobber here? **(FRASER has taken a bottle out of the booze box. Johnny Walker black label.)** HI! Don't even fuckin think it! That's my own for my own personal consumption. **(FRASER stares at him, opens the bottle and takes a big swig.)** Aye okay but that's your last.

FRASER: What I think is, that Janice'll go for you in a big way in those garments, Leonard.

LEONARD: Really. You think so.

FRASER: Show us your jacket on. **(LEONARD hesitates.)** Surprise Janice when she wakes up. **(LEONARD puts on the jacket.)** Show her what a difference a complete transformation can make.

LEONARD: Is it okay?

FRASER: Trousers. **(LEONARD puts them on.)** It's the same as you were saying yourself that Arbogast told you. A psychological transformation. You can never underestimate the effect that nice clothes have on a chick's perception of the real you, Leonard. How else do you imagine Willie Dobie'd be investing half his income on hand-printed ties and new suits.

LEONARD: That better?

FRASER: Shoes. **(LEONARD steps into the slip-ons.)**

LEONARD: Shoes and tie. Where's the tie?

FRASER: **(points)** Hangin out of your top pocket.

LEONARD: **(Finds it. It is an untied real bow-tie.)** Aw fuckin hell, how d'ye work these bastards?

FRASER: I've never worn one. Mind you, you're right, it needs the tie.

LEONARD: Trust Arbogast.

FRASER: Otherwise you just look like a half done tube.

LEONARD: Fuckin disastrous!

FRASER: Hoi Janice. Look at Leonard's half done tube outfit!

LEONARD: Hold on. Wait till I've got my tie tied.

He struggles with it. FRASER looks at him and laughs. LEONARD'S panic increases.

FRASER: What d'ye think, eh? Janice – cool as fuck eh?

LEONARD: Leave her you. Wait till I've got my . . .

FRASER: Janice!

LEONARD: This fucker fixed. Help me, you.

FRASER: I'm afraid personally I'm all thumbs and toes in the psychological department, pal.

LEONARD: Right then, well leave her. While I get Arbogast to fuckin fix this. And don't fuckin dare you wake her up, cause she needs her sleep. Or it's me you'll answer to. **(He heads for the lift, he points to the bottle of whisky in FRASER'S hand.)** And don't even so much as even think it, okay.

FRASER: Okay then Leonard.

LEONARD: That's okay then, Fraser. **(As the lift door closes)** Some haircut, right enough.

The lift ascends. FRASER waits for a couple of seconds then has another big slug of the whisky.

Scene 8   Bags

ARBOGAST is sweeping up. EVELYN is standing holding a bin liner open. Some music is playing – 'Stand By Me'. WILLIE DOBIE and HOLLY are doing a dance called 'The Stroll'. HOLLY started the dance and DOBIE has picked it up. He is chuffed with himself. EVELYN watches them, staring, clenched, miserable.

EVELYN: Look, she's all floppy, how come I'm no floppy, how come I feel as if I've been sharpened.

ARBOGAST: I've told you to hold your wheesht till we've finished, then I'll give you something to make you bloody FLOPPY!

DOBIE: **(without breaking step)** What, have the **(miming the word 'substances')** arrived yet?

ARBOGAST: Eh? . . . naw. I've got some . . . **(He pulls a wee pill bottle from his pocket.)**

DOBIE: What? Is that . . . **(He gestures with his head.)**

ARBOGAST: **(sniggers and holds the bottle away)** No . . . Willie, this is real drugs.

DOBIE: Eh?

ARBOGAST: You know, medical.

DOBIE: Pfshh . . .

ARBOGAST: Largactil.

DOBIE: Larg . . . The liquid cosh . . . ?

ARBOGAST: Aye, I mean I'm fine just now, you know, if I manage to steer clear of stressful situations.

DOBIE: Well as long as you know what you're doing. I've seen a documentary about the use of that stuff in high security prisons you know. **(To HOLLY)** Largactil.

HOLLY: Lovely

DOBIE: A great social leveller. Puts you on the same social level as escaped murderers haha. Eh Davey?

ARBOGAST: Aye, whatever you say, Willie, you're the boss.

DOBIE: Ach – away, don't be like that, we're a team. Eh girls. Come over here, ya scrawny old bastard. C'mere. Davey! **(ARBOGAST doesn't want to move.)** Davey – c'mere. **(ARBOGAST joins them.)** Swing your arms.

ARBOGAST: What?

DOBIE: Come on ya grumpy big stiffy – a bit of rhythm. Swing your fuckin arms. **(DOBIE gets back into the dance. ARBOGAST has no rhythm whatsoever.)** Oh look – The Link is no longer missing! Haha. Count! 1 an 2 an 3 an 4! Arbogast! Can you no count that high, c'mon – God's sake. Imagine you're twenty years younger. **(To HOLLY)** Mind you, he'd still be in his late forties, eh? **(To ARBOGAST)** Christ, Davey, this is not the stone age. You're like one of those dinosaurs with spikes out of a Million Years BC. Useless! **(He gives him a shove.)** Out the way and let the talent breathe. I realise the music's a bit fuckin contemporary for you, so you just get on with your sweepin up then.

HOLLY: **(stops dancing)** Do you ever feel like you used to be an Egyptian? And you were allowed to stay up all night and watch people from all over the world being sacrificed on a big slab. And you had a whole team of slaves covered in oil, building pyramids for you that you can lie in in the dark for thousands of years. And that one day you'll wake up and you'll be in the future like now and it'll all have just been something you dreamt. So your whole life suddenly makes sense. Have you ever felt that?

DOBIE: I have felt that, yes. I knew Arbogast when I was an Egyptian. He was a dung beetle haha. **(To HOLLY)** C'mon let's you and me go and take a look at the Nile, Princess. **(He leads HOLLY to a lift.)**

EVELYN: 'Princess', fucks sake. How come I get rigor mortis and she gets 'Princess'? How come I get lock-jaw and flashing lights behind my eyelids and menstrual cramp up the back of my spine and . . . and . . . and she gets to go and look at the Nile? Are you gonnae put some rubbish in this or have I to just stay here impersonating a receptacle till everybody's been and gone? **(ARBOGAST takes the top off his pill bottle and gives a tablet to EVELYN.)** Ta. How long do these take to work?

ARBOGAST: **(shrugs)** Depends.

EVELYN: On what?

ARBOGAST: Whether you're in a state of mild tension or a murderous rage.

EVELYN: I know. I think all that was just uncalled for. Does he think somebody can't have feelings just because they dance like a tube and they're dead old and they've got hair loss? I hate it when people are insensitive like that.

A lift arrives and LEONARD gets out.

LEONARD: **(to ARBOGAST)** Can you remember how you use one of these bastards?

EVELYN: It goes round your neck . . .

LEONARD: I KNOW it goes . . . Arbogast, can you remember how to tie one of these stupid old-fashioned . . . bow thingy fucks?

ARBOGAST: **(in a temper)** I can remember millions of things. I can remember my fuckin manners for a start as well as the Origins of the fuckin Universe. And I can remember when's the right time for getting your hole and when isn't. And I can remember exactly what I'm owed by folk, Leonard, and when to keep my gub shut. **(He pushes past LEONARD into the lift.)**

LEONARD: What's up with him? **(Pause)** What are you standing there holding that thing like that for?

EVELYN: I lumbered this guy who had a fetish about these. See in his room he had this bag full of polythene bags and for a sexual thrill he'd take a bag out of the bagful of polythene bags and then stick the bag full of polythene bags into the bag he'd taken out of the polythene bag full of polythene bags.

LEONARD: Eh? . . . what did he put in them?

EVELYN: Polythene bags. It was something to do with his childhood.

LEONARD: I loved my childhood.

EVELYN: Eh?

LEONARD: When I have a dream, and I'm walking about, then the handles on the doors are all at head height. I had the happiest childhood you can have. Every night in my dreams I'm a five-year-old again.

EVELYN: You're a five-year-old at the moment, never mind in your dreams

LEONARD: No really, cause it wasn't till I was older that I got my nervous skin complaint.

EVELYN: So what was it made you nervous?

LEONARD: It was . . . I think . . . I dunno I think . . . **(pause)** Lack of love. **(A brief, heart-stirringly emotional pause – then EVELYN falls about whooping with laughter.)** See I knew you'd just laugh. Cause by the time I was six I was the only one in my family who didn't have Tourette's syndrome. So when everybody else was gettin treatment and loads of attention in the local papers, I was gettin ignored as some sort of freaky failure of nature and it made my epidermis erupt in irritating patches . . . **(EVELYN is on her knees.)** At least it clears up when I've been puttin on my ointment! At least it doesn't say anything about me as a human being. **(EVELYN has keeled over.)** Aw fuck you too . . .

LEONARD heads for the lift in the huff. A pause. EVELYN lies there. She stops laughing. She twitches.

EVELYN: Fuck. Hello. Help me up. Could somebody help me up a bit please. Leonard. Help me up. I think I can learn to love you, Leonard.

Scene 9   Guilt

FRASER goes to the bucket he cut his hair into and pours half of the bottle of whisky into the bucket and then fills the bottle up with piss. He holds it up to inspect the colour.

JANICE: Leonard has this effect . . .

FRASER: Fuck, Janice, I thought you were sleepin . . .

JANICE: That's what I'm sayin, he has this effect . . .

FRASER: And I'm supposed to not disturb you.

JANICE: No I'm saying he has this effect that I feel I have to get some sleep as soon as he starts talking to me. Give me some of that, my mouth tastes foul.

FRASER: No way, Janice – this is Leonard's own personal supply for his own personal enjoyment and he trusts me to see nobody arses it.

JANICE: Anyway I wasn't really asleep, I was only kiddin so he wouldn't annoy me with his chit-chat. I thought you were scared of no man with your new haircut.

FRASER: Neither I am.

JANICE: Anyway I can't sleep. I've got such a thing as a conscience, you know, and so should you have too.

FRASER: What for?

JANICE: For having murdered Alec Sneddon, that's what for.

FRASER: I didnt 'murder' anybody. I wish everybody would stop saying . . . I have never 'murdered' a soul in my entire life!

JANICE: Well now you have. Thanks to Willie Dobie. You and me are worse criminals than pigs like Leonard and just as bad as murderers like Arbogast.

FRASER: Leonard nearly killed wee Raymond.

JANICE: Thanks to Willie Dobie.

FRASER: Stop saying 'Thanks to Willie Dobie' all the time, Janice. Thanks to Willie Dobie I'm a murderer and my best pal's had his toe chopped off. That's 'Thanks to Willie Dobie'.

JANICE: Your best pal?

FRASER: That Leonard left bleedin unconscious all over my bedroom rug.

JANICE: Your bedroom rug?

FRASER: And they said at the hospital they could have sewn it back on if I'd packed it in ice and kept it cold, except I couldn't find it cause Leonard's got it in a polythene bag as a memento. Even though I searched the whole of the flat.

JANICE: That Willie Dobie owns.

FRASER: So I went to see Willie Dobie, cause like Leonard says, you can always turn to Willie Dobie for a spot of help when you're in a bit of bother.

JANICE: Don't I know it. Cept it turns out to be him that's the source of all everybody's trouble. GOD! I need a drink. **(She chooses from amongst the bottles and has a wee drink.)** Do you know what I think, Fraser?

FRASER: No?

JANICE: I wish Alec Sneddon was here. I never lumbered him but he was dead nice to talk to.

FRASER: Huh. It was him got Raymond all involved in making drugs again.

JANICE: I know. I mean I know all that, that he was a drug . . . baron and everything. I'm not talking about that though. He was going to sort out all my rent problems with Dobie. He wasn't even scared of Dobie and that lot in the slightest. And now we've gone and murdered him. And I always had quite a nice time with Mad Alec – not special, just nice. I mean he never did anythin I wanted to kill him for. So maybe that makes it worse. Or better. I mean I hardly knew him really though. I don't know.

FRASER: I know.

JANICE: I mean if you look at it the other way, though, it wasn't really us that murdered him, even though it was.

FRASER: That's what I've been saying, Janice.

JANICE: Although WE did the ACT!

FRASER: Except I didn't know Alec Sneddon was in the back of the van.

JANICE: Hopefully Alec Sneddon didn't know he was in the back of the van either. Specially after you set it on fire.

FRASER: Look! I really don't want to keep getting reminded . . . All I want is my tickets to Ibiza and me and Raymond on the plane and we're out of here. Vamoose!

JANICE: Ibiza what? So housewives can stick pesetas down the front of your underpants?

FRASER: I'll have a costume!

JANICE: You've got a costume. You've got the haircut of a desperate man. Anyway what makes you think this lot are going to let you just Vamoose!

FRASER: Or you.

JANICE: Or me either except don't forget I'm the object of Leonard's deepest fantasies.

FRASER: Aye, except don't you forget Arbogast.

JANICE: Except Leonard is the son Arbogast never had, mind you, which makes him lucky he never had a son.

FRASER: So to stay in with Arbogast and Dobie you're prepared to lumber Leonard who you can't stand?

JANICE: No I can't. I fancy Leonard like I fancy cancer. I'd shag Alec Sneddon's charred corpse before I'd let Leonard rub his rash against me.

FRASER: **(really quite horrified)** That is just . . . sick!

JANICE: Sicker than setting somebody on fire?

FRASER: Will you stop . . . Bloody . . . That just hasn't sunk in. I've seen Leonard's skin condition.

JANICE: I'm sure it's no worse than the condition Alec Sneddon's is in. Anyway I don't have to lumber either of them and there's no need for you to be so crude.

FRASER: Oh I'm SORRY – well I take that back then.

JANICE: Thank you. I just feel very strongly that a new rent book and two plane tickets isn't really . . .

FRASER: Isn't really what?

JANICE: . . . Adequate. For you and me getting turned into murderers without anybody even asking our permission.

FRASER: Right. So. I don't understand what it is you're suggesting that we do. I mean I quite fancy the option of running away you know.

JANICE: What I'm saying is! . . . That we should fully consider our options. We should . . . we should . . . just . . . work out if there's something that we can both . . . get.

FRASER: So you think we should actually . . . 'get' something.

JANICE: I do. I definitely do think we should try to . . . to . . . 'get' . . . something.

FRASER: Uhuh. You're going to have to give me a for instance. **(Pause.)**

JANICE: Okay. I'm going to have to have another drink. Then I'll try to give you a for instance.

Scene 10   Animal Magnetism

On the roof. DOBIE is semi-astride the railing, popping another bottle of champagne. HOLLY is leaning on the railing. Both of them are a bit inflamed.

HOLLY: The bit I loved was the bit where she goes **(doing an American female accent)** 'I did it for you, Doc', and he goes 'Three years in the slammer, a man can't hide his feelings . . .'

DOBIE: I know . . .

HOLLY: And after that, the bit . . .

DOBIE: And the bit . . .

HOLLY: And the bit where . . . where . . . they're both . . .

DOBIE: Waiting for the train . . .

HOLLY: Yeah – where she gets his gun out the left luggage locker . . .

DOBIE: The pump action sawn-off . . .

HOLLY: And the bit where . . . she's running . . .

DOBIE: You can't get them here, you know, not even a replica.

HOLLY: . . . she's running in slow motion through the puddles outside the prison farm.

DOBIE: And he's waiting in slow motion inside the gates . . .

HOLLY: And then at the end it's dead good when he's . . .

DOBIE: When they hitch a lift in the back of that farmer's rubbish truck . . .

HOLLY: And they get to the border and she gets off the lorry to buy cigarettes and the baddies blow him to pieces and the poor Mexican farmer as well.

DOBIE: . . . I know I didn't like . . .

HOLLY: And she really suits it when she cries.

DOBIE: . . .yeah . . .

HOLLY: I sobbed buckets. Mind you she got the bag with all the money in it. So I suppose . . . I loved it.

DOBIE: **(takes a swig of his champagne and then faces her – excited)** I really didn't enjoy the end though. But up till then I loved it – I mean I really loved it! Cause – cause the guy, all the way through you know, he's got a Vision! I mean that bag of money doesn't just represent a bag of money! It's their future for both of them. Even though he gets blown up which I thought was absolutely gratuitous. And he's not afraid of . . . of . . . you know he never got scared by his responsibilities. Me! Look at me here – I mean I am Drowning in responsibilities. And . . . it's the same, you know . . . the hard fact is. The fundamental fact of the matter is if you don't have the strength to face your responsibilities then you drown. And nothing can change that simple, since time immemorial fact, as very many poor, sad, deluded people have learned to their ultimate cost. Guys with no sense . . . of themselves . . . their Destiny . . .

DOBIE is seriously thinking about trying a kiss. LEONARD arrives on the roof up the access ladder. LEONARD coughs.

DOBIE: What the fuck are you after? What the fuck is he wearing? What the fuck are you wearing, Leonard?

LEONARD: I was wondering if you . . . or . . . or . . . knew how you tied one of these . . . her.

DOBIE: Alec Sneddon had no sense of himself and that was the downfall of the man. **(To HOLLY)** Eh?

HOLLY: An animal.

DOBIE: **(to LEONARD)** Why don't you just get an elasticated one? **(To HOLLY)** The things that are put in a man's path to try him, eh?

HOLLY: And the things that an animal puts in a woman's path to . . . to . . .

LEONARD: I don't know if I can get an elasticated one.

DOBIE: Eh . . . ? God. Bring your neck over here then Leonard. And bring your bow-tie with it.

LEONARD does so. DOBIE ties his tie for him. HOLLY watches.

DOBIE: They say that's the ultimate in human trust, did you know that.

HOLLY: What?

LEONARD: What?

DOBIE: Allowing another man to place his hands around your throat, it goes back to the earliest beginning of civilisation when we were all still animals and everyone was at each other's throats the whole time. Men and women.

HOLLY: I only ever use my throat for swallowing.

DOBIE: **(to HOLLY)** And that's . . . you know that's as it should be. **(To LEONARD)** Meanwhile . . . Leonard. You should be able to feel the magnetic animal power in my fingertips and your personal feelings will be telling you whether or not you trust me. **(To HOLLY)** Just like the bit where the man can't hide his feelings after three years in the slammer. See what I mean . . . respect is what it all boils down to. **(To LEONARD)** It's good for me to know that, Leonard. That you trusted me to tie your tie for you. It means I know you can be trusted. On a very intimate level. It's one of the few ways you can read a man where he can't lie to you. **(He steps back. The tie is very badly knotted.)** And there's fuckin few of them my son. So we must pay heed to them when they happen.

LEONARD: **(to HOLLY)** Does it look okay?

HOLLY: It's a bit . . .

DOBIE: That is not the point! Whether it does or does not look okay. It's what the tying of the tie signifies to me about him in the most profound sense that matters. Not whether or not the bow-tie looks okay.

HOLLY: It looks a bit like an ordinary tie only you don't know how to tie it.

ARBOGAST also arrives on the roof.

DOBIE: I know that but the point is not about whether . . .

ARBOGAST: Excuse me a minute, Willie, I've got to . . .

DOBIE: WHAT!

ARBOGAST: Sorry, I'm saying . . .

DOBIE: WHAT?! Eh? Say it! What NOW?

A very uncomfortable pause. DOBIE is over-reacting and eveybody feels it.

HOLLY: Some party this is turning into. Shouting . . .

DOBIE: You are absolutely right, and I apologise, sir. You'd be well within your rights to give me a smack for that, Davey, that was right out of line. Or. **(He grins and goes into a boxing pose.)** You could try anyway, eh? Haha. **(He clips ARBOGAST with a couple of jokey slap punches.)** I'd like to see you give it a try, eh, Davey. Square goes, you and me, and the best man's the one with all his own teeth at the end. Though that puts you out the runnin from the off, eh, Davey.

He drops the boxing pose and turns serious. He marches to ARBOGAST and takes his elbow.

DOBIE: What can I say, sir – I'm under a lot of pressure here, so we all have to make allowances, come on down to my office and we'll get everything sorted out.

He leads ARBOGAST down the stairs – leaving LEONARD awkward with HOLLY.

LEONARD: Pair of lethal bastards, eh?

HOLLY: Who?

LEONARD: That pair. I'm telling you there's no way Arbogast would stand for that if he didn't . . . you know . . . I mean it's like . . .

HOLLY: Like what?

LEONARD: Well I know him and I've seen him when he's got his dander up and it's just . . . phwoof!

HOLLY: So?

LEONARD: So I'm only saying, if either of them ever took exception. I mean I've seen Arbogast . . . I mean I didn't even know what a tracheotomy was.

HOLLY: And now you do?

LEONARD: Yeah. Same as an appendectomy apparently only on your throat. That's how you can tell they respect each other cause I've seen Arbogast.

HOLLY: Oh. Right.

LEONARD: Or else it would just be mayhem.

HOLLY: Uhuh.

LEONARD: It would be just . . . just . . . like what Willie was saying when he had his hands round my neck about how we're really all just animals. That's what it would be like. Only probably more psychological than animals. You know with real human blood.

Scene 11　Late Afternoon of the Living Dead

FRASER and JANICE in the basement. Both are perked up, excited and a bit pished. The little tranny is playing. JANICE is singing and keeping time, bottle in hand. FRASER is dancing and singing along. They argue about the lyrics without dropping the rhythm of the song.

JANICE: Aga do do do. Push my apple pull my tree . . . Aga do . . .

FRASER: Pineapple! . . . do do . . .

JANICE: Pineapple?

BOTH: DA DA DEE-DEE-DEE-DEE-DEE! AGA DO DO DO PUSH PINEAPPLE

JANICE: Pull my tree . . .

FRASER: Grind Coffee . . .

JANICE: What's that one?

(FRASER stops as well.)

FRASER: Grind Co-Ffee.

JANICE: Uh?

FRASER: Janice, the words are 'Pull pineapple grind coffee!' . . .

The lift arrives and the doors open. EVELYN stands there. She is exceedingly dazed and incapable of getting out of the lift.

FRASER: Not . . . 'Push my apple pull my tree' for fucks sake. I mean what is it you think this song's about in the first place?

JANICE: Sex!

FRASER: Well you're wrong.

JANICE: It's you that's moving your pelvis.

FRASER: I am not moving my . . . I'm dancing. It's not about sex, it's about . . . working on a plantation or something. It's traditional. **(To EVELYN, who is standing in the lift with her mouth hanging open, drooling lightly and staring)** Isn't it?

JANICE: Keugh. Traditional?

FRASER: That the natives invented.

JANICE: What natives?

FRASER: The natives that invented the song in the first place that they used to sing when they were working on the . . .

JANICE: Bucks Fizz?

FRASER: It's not . . .

JANICE: Cause they never worked on a plantation . . .

FRASER: It isn't by . . .

JANICE: Unless it was in one of their videos that I never saw . . .

FRASER: IT ISN'T BY BUCKS FUCKING FIZZ!!! Sorry. The song

is a song about voodoo and how you can . . . you can numb yourself to the daily drudgery of digging up coconuts on a plantation by swallowing this potion that makes you into a kind of zombie that does whatever anybody tells you all the time even if it's against your will normally . . .

EVELYN: Sex slaves!

FRASER: . . . Yes. Well . . . maybe. Not necessarily.

JANICE: You don't dig coconuts . . .

FRASER: Whatever . . . bananas then.

EVELYN: Is this the party?

JANICE: **(quietly)** I'm fairly sure you don't dig bananas either . . .

FRASER: No this isn't . . . are you okay?

EVELYN: I'm sick.

JANICE: I know. I was sick earlier.

EVELYN: I'm gonnae BE sick.

FRASER: Do you want me to smoothe your brow?

EVELYN: Eh?

JANICE: He's dead sympathetic. Really. He really is.

FRASER gets the poly bag he wiped his hair on and snaps it open for EVELYN to use to be sick in. He goes towards her.

EVELYN: I'm not a sex slave.

JANICE: He's not saying . . . have you been drinking?

EVELYN: I've had medicine. **(She clocks the polythene bag, then she looks at FRASER and JANICE.)** Perverts! **(She collapses.)**

JANICE: I told you that song wasn't just about coconuts.

Scene 12   Respect

DOBIE and ARBOGAST in DOBIE'S office. There is a desk and an anglepoise lamp.

ARBOGAST: I mean you're right and I cannot disagree, Willie, she's a lovely lookin doll.

DOBIE: She's a princess. And also a sense of humour.

ARBOGAST: Not to be laughed at, Willie.

DOBIE: I know and . . .

ARBOGAST: Can I ask you something?

DOBIE: Fire away, Davey, s'what I'm here for.

ARBOGAST: Have you got things sorted out for this evening?

DOBIE: You know me better than that, son.

ARBOGAST: I know.

DOBIE: Exactly.

ARBOGAST: So what I'm saying is . . . concentrate here because I'm thinking hard about all this myself.

DOBIE: Oh – 'CONCENTRATE!' . . . no on you go . . .

ARBOGAST: Because somebody has to. I want to know if the folk who've got invited . . .

DOBIE: Of course . . .

ARBOGAST: The important folk . . .

DOBIE: Uhuh.

ARBOGAST: That a lot hinges on . . .

DOBIE: **(pouring champagne into his glass)** Our vision, Davey.

ARBOGAST: . . . and those special guests that are going to distribute our product upon whom we depend . . .

DOBIE: A shared dependancy. Haha.

ARBOGAST: Uhuh. That when they turn up eventually, they're going to be met with a . . .

DOBIE: One whale of a time.

ARBOGAST: With a semblance of. With something not just . . . With all the ground work done and the problems sorted out.

DOBIE: **(proffering a glass)** You joinin me?

ARBOGAST: Willie. Can we talk straight?

DOBIE: Well I can, Davey, but with regard to yourself I have some doubts . . .

ARBOGAST steps towards DOBIE, fast and angry.

ARBOGAST: Well you can cut that shite out for a start – it's not one of your idiot fuckin dolies your talking to here.

DOBIE squares up to deal with this insubordination.

DOBIE: Now just you steady on a wee minute here . . .

ARBOGAST goes Chernobyl meltdown on him, grabbing DOBIE'S throat in one hand and his scrotum in the other.

ARBOGAST: Don't fucking steady on a wee minute here me, ya little prick! I have had enough of your arsing around to last me! If you fuck me up in this I will rip out your spinal column. I will swap the brains in your skull with the shite from your bowel. And vice versa! Now is that fathomable for you?

DOBIE nods. They pause. ARBOGAST dusts him down a little.

ARBOGAST: Eh? Good God man.

DOBIE: No, you're right. That's perfectly fathomable and I apologise. **(He offers his hand.)** It's not that I don't respect you, cause I do. Mutual respect.

ARBOGAST: **(He pauses)** Willie. Keep things simple eh? **(takes DOBIE'S hand but doesn't shake it, just clamps it in a superhuman vice grip.)** Now answer me a question or two. Are you or are you not the man in charge?

DOBIE: **(can hardly think for the pain)** Am I or am I not . . . ?

ARBOGAST: . . . the man in charge.

DOBIE: I . . .

ARBOGAST: . . . Yes?

DOBIE: . . . am.

ARBOGAST: You are. Good. Excellent. We know where we stand. Have you, as the man in charge – Seen to your responsibilities?

DOBIE: **(can't believe the pain)** Pffew . . . eh . . .

ARBOGAST: What I mean by that, Willie, is . . .

DOBIE: Uhuh.

ARBOGAST: **(giggles)** It's fuckin funny really, just look at you, ya trumped up wee jerk. **(He releases DOBIE'S hand, leaving DOBIE on his knees.)** I'll tell you some news, shall I, kiddo.

DOBIE: Uhuh.

ARBOGAST: I mean you've worked dead hard and done well for yourself, nobody's denying you that. There's all your tenements chock full of dolies paying you DHSS money and doing you favours — I mean that's all very commendable. And you've saved up and bought this place. And you've got your own wee tame chemist to make the stuff for you. And you've got Alec Sneddon out the way. Now. Do you know what that all adds up to?

DOBIE: Tell me?

ARBOGAST: A very useful foundation. And so. See I need to know if you're up to your responsibilities. That if you set something in motion you won't let it all just fall apart on your head. On everybody's head. Are we speaking our language?

DOBIE: We are. That is my language you're speaking. I'm just not a hundred per cent sure what you're actually talking about.

ARBOGAST: The thing that has to be done. The two pests in the basement. Now in so far as I took care of things up to here as YOU requested, you now find yourself with the opportunity to tie the whole business up in the one go.

DOBIE: That is the way it seems, isn't it?

ARBOGAST: So it is.

DOBIE: Where is it the boy wants his tickets to again?

ARBOGAST: **(patiently)** No no no no no no. **(He goes to DOBIE and puts his hands on his shoulders.)** No no no no no Willie. Listen to me. You go out to the car park . . .

DOBIE: Should I not be . . .

ARBOGAST: Just! Listen to me a minute.

He holds up a bunch of car keys. DOBIE takes them.

ARBOGAST: Under the front seat of my Volvo you'll find a sawn-off shotgun and you go down to the basement and you shoot the boy first and then you shoot the doll . . .

DOBIE: . . . shoot . . .

ARBOGAST: In the head, then burn the bits.

DOBIE: . . . shoot . . . **(He gulps.)** . . . I could never . . . then burn . . . I couldn't . . .

ARBOGAST: You're a big boy, you'll manage.

DOBIE: Davey . . . Davey I could never . . . You couldn't . . . For God's sake! **(He cackles.)** You're some man, Davey, I mean everybody knows . . .

ARBOGAST: Everybody knows the doll's been seeing Sneddon and now he's burned to death in the back of his van. And the boy's been doin his nut about his tickets. And the boy was in her room the night Sneddon disappeared. And everybody knows what a mad dog Alec was. So he found out and he would've murdered the boy. But the love birds murdered him first before they ran away together to . . .

DOBIE: **(softly)** Ibiza.

ARBOGAST: Ibiza! The very same. **(He goes to the lift.)** And who can blame them for that. A very lovely place this time of the year despite what you read. I've been there myself. Under the front seat, Willie. **(He stands in the lift waiting for DOBIE'S acquiescence.)** . . . Willie?

DOBIE: Under the front seat. Shoot them in the head. Burn them.

ARBOGAST: I knew it. Same language all along. You just need it spelt out a bit.

The door closes. The lift descends.

66

Scene 13   Spleen

In the basement. FRASER, JANICE, HOLLY, LEONARD and EVELYN. JANICE and FRASER are leaning over EVELYN. HOLLY is a bit spaced. FRASER and JANICE sit EVELYN up. Her face and arms are covered in red blotches.

LEONARD: Is she breathing?

JANICE: She's wheezing a bit.

HOLLY: I knew he was contagious.

FRASER: It's an allergic reaction.

HOLLY: Well it's not as though we've been stuffing our faces with prawns is all I'm saying. So who knows.

LEONARD: I never laid a finger on . . . anyway I'm not bloody contagious, you so will you stop making remarks, your pal's dying.

HOLLY: Okay. I'll stop if you stop. Anyway it's her own fault, she's always doin this to me at parties. So where did she get the spots?

LEONARD: Fuck knows.

HOLLY: Who're you callin fuck nose, pizza features. **(She giggles.)** Sorry, that's just the drugs I took making me say things I don't mean again, they were doin that before.

JANICE: Anyway. She'll be okay when she gets better.

LEONARD: **(fetches the Johnny Walker whisky bottle)** Give her a glug of this, that'll buck her up.

FRASER: Don't give her . . . no you shouldn't give somebody alcohol when they've got food poisoning.

LEONARD: No?

HOLLY: We've not had any food. In fact I'm bloody famished. Has anybody got any?

LEONARD: Grub? Aye sure doll.

He gets the bag with RAYMOND'S toe out of his pocket and passes it to HOLLY, who is nicely surprised by his generosity.

HOLLY: Ta. What is it? Looks foul. Looks like a bit of sausage gone rancid.

LEONARD winks at FRASER as he unscrews the whisky bottle.

LEONARD: They're lovely. Marks and Spencers do them. We are talkin taste bud sensation here.

He takes a slug of the whisky as HOLLY pops Raymond's toe in her mouth. For a second they eye each other, then HOLLY starts chewing and LEONARD swallows. He retches. HOLLY takes the toe out of her mouth and looks at it.

HOLLY: They're a bit chewy. I don't know if I like them. **(To JANICE)** Try it?

JANICE: I'll save it for . . .

LEONARD: Fucks sake . . . who's been . . . has somebody been . . .

FRASER: Oh God, she's stopped breathing, quick, undo her . . .

EVELYN sits up and looks round as the lift arrives and ARBOGAST gets out.

EVELYN: Touch me and you die, I've got the whirling spinnies, I'll be fine when I've . . .

A pause. She plonks back down again.

ARBOGAST: I thought you three were supposed to be upstairs sweeping up, what's the matter with her?

JANICE: She'll be fine if she gets a breath of air.

ARBOGAST: So she will as well. Why don't you take the lassie outside, Leonard?

HOLLY: **(going to the lift)** Yeah come on . . . Bring her up on the roof, it's lovely up there. You can see all the way to Ancient Egypt.

LEONARD: Me?

FRASER: Yeah, you're security, you're meant to be in charge of things like this.

LEONARD: You're right. No problem.

He picks EVELYN up in a fireman's lift.

LEONARD: **(to HOLLY)** Gonnae get the lift, fuck nose.

HOLLY: **(a beat)** Only cause she's my best pal, but Willie Dobie'll kill you if I get a rash off your poisonous sausage, plooky. **(As they head for the lift)** I meant that thing you got from Marks and Spencers, not that thing you've got in your underpants.

LEONARD: I got my underpants from Marks and Spencers as well . . .

The lift departs.

FRASER: **(to ARBOGAST)** Right then, have you got my tickets?

JANICE: And my rent book.

ARBOGAST: Willie's sortin all that out, he's good at that kinda thing. Paper work.

JANICE: I want to ask you something.

ARBOGAST: Uhuh.

JANICE: As a for instance, if somebody just asked you, just hypothetically speaking, how much would you say it would cost them to pay to get somebody else murdered.

FRASER: Janice . . .

JANICE: Just off the top of your head.

ARBOGAST: Off the top of my head? Depends.

JANICE: **(to FRASER)** See I told you.

FRASER: **(to ARBOGAST)** I told her you wouldn't have the faintest clue what she's talking about.

ARBOGAST: Absolutely. I think Willie Dobie's your man for that sort of question.

FRASER: That's what I said.

ARBOGAST: Just hypothetically speaking of course.

FRASER: Sure. So would he know as well how much it would cost to get somebody beaten up so badly that they have to get taken straight to the hospital with bits chopped off them?

ARBOGAST: You know, Fraser, that haircut of yours makes you look as though you've had one half of your head shot away.

FRASER: Does it?

ARBOGAST: It suits you as well.

JANICE: My Uncle Neil got shot in Northern Ireland by a soldier. Mind you my Uncle Neil was a soldier as well. So I suppose it must have been an accident. Mind you, knowing my Uncle Neil . . . He's no got any spleen. He says it was like, if you can imagine lying stretched out on your back and somebody stands above you with a pick-axe and then swings the point of it into your stomach as hard as they can, then that's what it felt like. Cept he was standing up when it happened. And then he got given a really nice medal.

ARBOGAST: **(He giggles, genuinely impressed with JANICE.)** My my, you're a fly wee tinker right enough, aren't you. What you're askin me is what it's worth to our man Willie Dobie to buy the silence of you two hardened murderers in the light of recent events. Eh?

FRASER: Hang on, hang on, she's saying no such thing. 'Buy the silence.' Who said anything about anything like that? She's just pointing out that what we did for Willie was worth . . .

ARBOGAST: Worth what? All going to jail for. Getting murdered yourselves . . .

FRASER: . . . two one-way tickets to Ibiza and a new rent book.

JANICE: **(to ARBOGAST)** If Willie Dobie knew anybody he could get to murder us, then he wouldn't have had to get us to murder Alec Sneddon would he? Mister Smart Arse.

FRASER: Janice, you go on about this nonsense more than anybody I've ever met in my life. **(To ARBOGAST)** Don't listen to her, she's daft.

JANICE: I didn't volunteer to get involved in Willie Dobie's orgy of death did I?

FRASER: Exactly, so shut up about it. Harping on all the time. What happened to make-up and babies?

JANICE: Oh right I'll just talk to myself about make-up and babies and you pair talk to each other about getting your hole and chopping people up?

FRASER: When have I mentioned a word about getting my hole?

JANICE: You don't have to mention it, just take a look at the way you were dancing with me a wee while ago.

FRASER: Eh?

JANICE: And consider what your pelvis was up to. Cause it was an obscenity.

FRASER: MY pelvis?

JANICE: Thrusting at me.

FRASER: Oh not just thrusting but At You.

JANICE: Right in my face.

FRASER: Aye in your dreams doll.

JANICE: Huh! In my worst nightmares you mean.

ARBOGAST: Ach, I don't know. **(He goes to the lift.)** Stick him in some clothes and fix his hairdo. **(ARBOGAST leaves.)**

FRASER: Not as bad a nightmare as my worst nightmare.

JANICE: You've got no idea about worst nightmares, Fraser, cause you've got no imagination.

FRASER: And you have.

JANICE: Yes I have. My brain is almost eighty-five per cent imaginary, so you can take that back. About not as bad a nightmare as your worst nightmare, cause there's guys'd kill for the privelege pal – so don't give me 'What my pelvis' in that tone. Cause I know from years of experience that that is a totally phoney tone. Pal.

FRASER: I think you . . . has it never . . .

JANICE: Since I was fourteen.

FRASER: Listen.

JANICE: Swine like you undoing all my buttons with their eyeballs.

FRASER: I've never even glanced at your bloody buttons.

JANICE: Ach don't come it, Fraser. You've got the mind of a sewer. Exactly the same as all the Leonards and the Willie Dobies . . .

FRASER: I am not the same as . . . Listen you! And your eighty-five per cent imaginary brain. Why do you imagine it was that it was me who took Raymond to the hospital and sat and held his hand while they dressed his stump and put bandages all round his face where he'd got drilled and then went out and got him his favourite wine gums and then sat and waited while they took him away to X-ray him for broken ribs and ruptured organs because some fat scabby bastard had been kickin him . . .

JANICE: **(seeing him getting upset, not sure why)** . . . Okay don't . . .

FRASER: **(almost tearful)** 'Don't' – what are you on about 'don't' – you can't just 'don't '. . .

JANICE: Hoi Fraser . . .

FRASER: Oh you mean hoi, Fraser don't get upset – eh? – Fraser don't cry.

JANICE: No I just meant, I meant don't . . . You . . . I'm sorry, you said he was your pal, I didn't know you meant he was . . . I'm sorry, Fraser.

FRASER: **(laughs)** Do you know what's funny . . .

JANICE: What?

FRASER: I mean Alec Sneddon was really scary and everything and Raymond and me were both terrified of him but one night at Blisters he came into his office and Raymond had been waiting for him for hours, and me and Raymond were killing some time, you know and he came in and I thought . . .

73

Fuck he's gonnae demolish us both and Sneddon goes . . .
'Boys – your bodies are your own. Just don't get any dribbles
on my nice linoleum. And feed Delilah and put the lights off
when you've finished.'

JANICE: 'Delilah?'

FRASER: His boa constrictor.

JANICE: Oh. **(Pause)** Is that like a python or something.

FRASER: Yup.

JANICE: And he had one as a pet?

FRASER nods.

JANICE: In his office. **(Pause)** I never knew that. **(Pause)** I wish
we hadn't killed him.

FRASER: I know. I wish we hadn't as well.

JANICE: Willie Dobie said he was his pal and I'd to entertain him
with my wit and charm. And see the first time, at Blisters –
he didn't hardly look at me. And then the week after that I
was sitting by myself and some sweaty fat guy bought me a
Taboo who I told to get raffled after a minute and Alec came
over and said 'Is this guy bothering you', and the guy bolted
and we had a nice chat. And then the week after that he
remembered my name and got me a basket of
complimentary buffalo wings that I could have sworn was
chicken but I didn't want to offend him. And we had a dance.
And I started to like him but I was a bit pished so when he
said would I like to come to his office and have a look at his
big snake I got the wrong end of the stick and I thought he
was just as bad as all the rest.

**She lights a ciggy. Her fingers are trembling. FRASER has
to help her with the lighter.**

JANICE: Fraser, I never knew he had a boa constrictor. I honestly never knew that. I thought he was just being a pig.

FRASER: He doted on Delilah.

JANICE has got quivery lip.

JANICE: I think that's so beautiful.

FRASER: What?

JANICE: The name. Delilah. And everything. Being devoted to a reptile. Except we never really talked. And then last night he ran me home.

JANICE is a bit tearful.

FRASER: Janice . . . don't. I mean . . . Have a Mirage.

JANICE: Thanks, Fraser. **(She has some Mirage.)** Oh God – he was a lovely dancer.

FRASER: I know. I saw him dancing. He's a great dancer.

JANICE: Do you know something, Fraser – he never even tried it on with me in the slightest. Never even so much as a feel. He never even tried to come up for a cup of coffee after he run me home in his van last night.

FRASER: He might've though, maybe, if I hadn't burned him to death in the back. You know, next weekend.

JANICE: Well there's no gonnae be any next weekend, is there.

FRASER: . . . No there's not.

FRASER has some Mirage too.

Scene 14 Vertigo

EVELYN is clinging on to the metal ventilation outlet. HOLLY and LEONARD are on the roof with her.

HOLLY: Evelyn, if you don't open your eyes . . .

EVELYN: If I open my eyes I'll fall.

HOLLY: Will you open your eyes and let go of the ventilation outlet and come and get some fresh air.

EVELYN: I've got fresh air here.

HOLLY: That air's not fresh, it's filthy, everybody in there's been inhaling it for ages.

EVELYN: **(very determined)** I am not letting go of the ventilation outlet. Ever. If I open my eyes I will get sucked to the edge of the roof and fall off. I know I will!

LEONARD: You'd better be careful about that cause we're six floors up . . .

EVELYN whimpers.

LEONARD: That'll be vertigo. It's a psychological complaint. Like my eczema only in your brain. And there's jaggy cement and scaffolding at the bottom to land on as well.

Another whimper from EVELYN.

HOLLY: Shut it you. **(From the edge of the roof)** Look! You won't get sucked off and fall.

LEONARD: Plus rats and mice and slugs and spiders.

HOLLY: **(yelps and steps away from the edge of the roof)** Slugs?

LEONARD: That'll be a psychological fear of slugs.

DOBIE appears at the top of the ladder.

DOBIE: Leonard stop fartin about with the fuckin floozy and get your arse into my office. Pronto!

LEONARD: Straight away, Willie, sir.

LEONARD goes to follow DOBIE. He turns back to the girls.

LEONARD: Don't worry about the slugs, they're all in your mind. **(HOLLY winces.)** Apart from the big slimy one on the back of your leg there. **(HOLLY jumps.)**

EVELYN: **(still clinging on with her eyes screwed shut)** Leave her alone ya scratchy big bloody big bastard big fuck pig!

LEONARD: **(leaving the roof)** Tourette's Syndrome. Another terrible mental affliction.

EVELYN: Holly come over here and cuddle me, there's no slugs!

HOLLY: 'Floozy'. Did you hear that? 'Effing floozy'! What happened to pumpkin and petal and princess?

Scene 15 · Delegation

LEONARD and DOBIE in DOBIE'S office.

LEONARD: So honestly I wasn't chattin her up – either of them. I was only . . .

DOBIE: You've no need to explain your private emotions to me, son. You and me know a thing or two about one another that means we don't have to go into particular details the whole time because there's a trust that exists that goes beyond that, you understand?

LEONARD: Perfectly, I couldn't put it . . .

DOBIE: And I know for instance that if I say to you, and this is a famous quote, Leonard, if I say, 'God gonnae grant me the serenity to be able to . . . to . . . change those things that I can-NOT accept and the wisdom to know how to . . . to . . .do it', then you know exactly what I'm referring to. Am I right?

LEONARD: You are perfectly . . . one hundred per cent.

DOBIE: Right. What?

LEONARD: Uhuh. Ehmmm . . .

DOBIE: That we're all lumbered if people shirk their responsibilities.

LEONARD: As if I'd do that.

DOBIE: Which brings us neatly to the matter in hand.

LEONARD: Right. Fire away.

DOBIE: I want you to go to the car, Leonard.

LEONARD: That's not a problem, Willie, no sooner said than . . .

DOBIE: Go to the car and look under the front seat.

LEONARD: **(pulls out the keys to Willie's Mercedes, flourishes them and heads off)** No problem whatsoever.

DOBIE: Wait a minute, son.

LEONARD: What.

DOBIE: **(pulling out the keys to Arbogast's Volvo, patiently explaining)** I don't want you to go to my Mercedes, I want you to go to Arbogast's Volvo.

LEONARD: **(grabs the keys)** Oh. Right. **(He heads off again. He stops.)** Why?

DOBIE: Why do you think, Leonard.

LEONARD: Eh . . . to get something.

DOBIE: Yes. What?

LEONARD: I don't know. Whatever's under the seat.

DOBIE: Which is what?

LEONARD: Which is . . . I don't know.

DOBIE: Which is a box of cartridges and a double-barrelled shotgun with the ends of the barrels sawn off so that you can hide it under your jacket and not miss when you shoot somebody with it at close range, that's what.

LEONARD: Right. **(He heads off again then stops.)** What do you want one of them for? I never even knew we had one of them.

DOBIE: I don't want one of them. You do.

LEONARD: Me?

DOBIE: You, Leonard.

LEONARD: How?

DOBIE: Because unless you want to kill him with your bare hands you're going to need it to blow Mister Arbogast's brains out. That's how.

Scene 16   Splatter

JANICE and FRASER in the basement. ARBOGAST comes in with an armful of bin bags and a mop and a bucket and a shovel.

ARBOGAST: You pair still here.

JANICE: What do you expect, we've still not seen Willie Dobie, have we?

ARBOGAST: That's who I was lookin for too, hen, I thought he might need this lot.

FRASER: How, you havin the party in the basement?

ARBOGAST: Very funny, doll. Best to have the whole shooting match cleaned up and no mess to upset the party-goers, don't you both think? Listen, I'll just dump this stuff the now and when Willie comes in you can tell him it's right here for him to get a shift on with before he sorts out your problems for you once and for all. You do that for me?

He dumps the gear. He picks up LEONARD'S bottle of whisky. LEONARD arrives in the lift.

ARBOGAST: Leonard, son. **(He holds out his hand.)** Car keys!

LEONARD: Eh?

LEONARD stands rooted, a set of car keys in either pocket, a hand jammed in with them.

ARBOGAST: The keys to the car.

LEONARD: Eh?

ARBOGAST: Leonard, give me the keys to Willie's car now would you. Please. Now. And don't get me demented, son.

LEONARD: Right. Willie's car keys.

He gingerly extracts a trembly fist containing a set of car keys. He holds the keys out, still clenched in his mitt.

LEONARD: What do you want the keys to Willie's car for?

ARBOGAST: Because. **(He taps his watch.)** Time to visit the chemist and pick up the big prescription.

LEONARD: No, I'm fine really, my skin's almost completely . . .

ARBOGAST: Leonard.

LEONARD: Oh right. That prescription. Sorry.

He opens the fist. Massive relief – he gives them to ARBOGAST. ARBOGAST leaves. LEONARD dances about in a paroxysm of nerves.

LEONARD: Ayargh . . . !

FRASER: What's up with your pus! Is your eczema itching?

LEONARD forces FRASER onto his back on the palettes and goes to drill his eyeballs.

LEONARD: I've told you it is pronounced eczema. It's nervous.
  And it's not my fault. **(He pulls the trigger of the drill.)**
  Fuck!

JANICE: Leonard! Don't! Leave him, he didn't mean that. It'll
  clear up when you're older.

He releases the trigger.

LEONARD: Fuck! Janice. Willie Dobie's gone daft.

JANICE: **(to FRASER)** You okay Fraser? **(FRASER signals
  he's okay.)** You're a big pig Leonard.

LEONARD: No Janice, help me. He says I'm supposed to find
  Arbogast and . . .

JANICE: You just found him a minute ago.

LEONARD: No Janice, listen! He says I've not to just find him,
  I've got to get a sawn-off shotgun from out the car and THEN
  find him and then I've got to shoot him with it.

FRASER: **(from the floor)** Right. Okay that's it. Stuff your ticket
  I'm going home!

JANICE: He says WHAT?

LEONARD: Do you think he's kiddin me, eh? He must be.

JANICE: Kidding you?

LEONARD: As a test.

JANICE: He told you to shoot Arbogast with a gun.

LEONARD: Yes.

JANICE: With a real gun? Shoot him.

LEONARD: That's what I said.

FRASER has managed to sneak over to the lift. He presses the button and waits.

LEONARD: Then I realised on the way to the car it must be a test you know? To see what I'm made of. Psychologically. So I thought – brilliant. I'll just get the gun out the car and then I'll go back to check with Willie and then I'll have passed the test, only then I thought, fuck! What if Arbogast finds out I actually went to get the gun, he'll fuckin murder me, what the fuck does Dobie think he's playin at, and then when I looked in the car there wasn't any gun anyway. **(The lift arrives and FRASER hauls the door open.)** Fuck!

LEONARD belts after FRASER.

JANICE: No Leonard wait . . . I've got it, Leonard.

LEONARD: **(from the lift doorway)** What?

JANICE: Show him your toe.

LEONARD: I'll show him my toe alright, I'll kick his fuckin eyeballs out!

LEONARD goes into the lift. The drill whirrs again and FRASER squeals in terror. Random banging noises.

JANICE: The toe you chopped off the student!

Pause. Then LEONARD emerges from the lift with FRASER under his arm, all hands on the drill, FRASER'S eyes screwed shut.

LEONARD: Eh?

JANICE: Well if all he wants is to test you to see if you're up to it psychologically all you have to do is show him the toe you chopped off the pharmacy student and he'll know he can rely on you.

LEONARD: **(dropping FRASER)** Janice that's brilliant. **(Pause)** Fuck!

JANICE: What?

LEONARD: I gave it to that bird that's terrified of slugs and she ate it.

JANICE: No she never, she spat it out and said she'd have it later. She's most probably still got it.

LEONARD: Janice you are brilliant. **(Huge pause. The biggest moment of LEONARD'S life.)** I . . . love you . . . Janice.

She's utterly and absolutely blank. LEONARD dies inside, then heads back to the lift. A stone killer to the depths of his soul.

LEONARD: See if that bitch has eaten it I'll fuckin kill her. **(He dives into the lift and leaves.)**

FRASER: Oh that's great, thanks Janice.

JANICE: What?

FRASER: First he chops Raymond's toe off and kicks his head and his organs in then he kicks my head in then you go and tell him how to get his bacon saved using my best pal's chopped off toe.

83

JANICE: So would you rather I just let him keep kicking your head in, I told you he was a pig.

FRASER: **(absolutely fucked and past caring)** I wouldn't care. I don't give a toss any more. And I'm bloody freezing as well. I am a frozen freezer.

JANICE: Fraser.

FRASER: What?

JANICE: **(producing the bag)** I've got the toe.

FRASER: Oh. Right. So.

JANICE: So you can give it back to Raymond.

FRASER: Right. So I can.

JANICE: And you can tell him how you got revenge for him from Willie Dobie.

FRASER: **(pause)** . . . Janice . . .

JANICE: Cause you're in love with him, aren't you.

FRASER: In love with him?

JANICE: In love with him.

FRASER: . . . Yes.

JANICE: And I'll help you.

FRASER: How?

JANICE: Because I was in love with Alec Sneddon, that's how.

They head for the lift.

Scene 17   Wine Gums

HOLLY and EVELYN on the roof. EVELYN is still clinging to the ventilation outlet. She has has Raymond's tortured spectacles in one hand. HOLLY is looking over the edge. She is clutching a small polythene bag.

EVELYN: Do you think Leonard's going to be okay?

HOLLY: Definitely not. There's stuff coming out of his head.

EVELYN: Holly don't. I had that earlier.

HOLLY: It's all over the jaggy cement. It looks like slugs but I think it's his brains.

EVELYN: I think that happened to me earlier as well.

HOLLY: I know Evelyn, but that was psychological. The sluggy stuff's Leonard's real physical brains. It's a horrible mess down there.

EVELYN: Holly, don't look down then.

A pause. They look at each other. Then HOLLY looks down again.

EVELYN: Who was the wee chubby guy in the cagoule with the limp?

HOLLY: And the can of petrol?

EVELYN: Uhuh.

HOLLY: I don't know. I thought him and Leonard were chums.

EVELYN: If they were chums he wouldn't have pushed Leonard off the roof would he?

HOLLY: Depends. Maybe they'd had a row about something.

EVELYN: What's in the polythene bag the chubby boy gave you,

Holly?

HOLLY: **(holding the polythene bag at arm's length)** I don't know. **(She has a feel.)** They're squishy. I'm scared to look. What did he give you?

EVELYN: Some specs.

HOLLY: Put them on.

EVELYN: I'll put them on if you look in the bag.

HOLLY opens the bag and peeks in.

EVELYN: What are they? Eyeballs?

HOLLY: They're not eyeballs, Evelyn. They're wine gums.

EVELYN: Thank God, eh?

HOLLY: Try the specs. **(EVELYN puts the specs on.)** You probably have to open your eyes, Evelyn.

EVELYN: Fuck! That's incredible.

HOLLY: What?

EVELYN: **(stepping away from the ventilation outlet)** The view from up here. I've never seen anything like it. I can see right through you, Holly, all the way into outer space. **(She looks at her arms.)** And my blotches has gone as well and everything. Holly?

HOLLY: What?

EVELYN: You look like an Egyptian Princess. Holly?

HOLLY: What?

EVELYN: Come and we'll just sit here and hold hands and look at the stars and we can wait here till it starts to get light and then we can watch the sun come up. Eh?

HOLLY: Okay. I've never seen that.

She sits next to EVELYN. They wait for the sun to come. Time passes.

EVELYN: We'll give it another five minutes, then we'll fuck off and get chips.

Scene 18   Stardust

WILLIE DOBIE in the main party area. Sweeping up the floor himself. Some music playing. The lift opens and JANICE and FRASER arrive.

DOBIE: You the exotic dancer, that is one hell of a rotten costume you've got there, son. What is it you do? A get dressed tease act. Haha.

JANICE: It's not a costume. First. He wants his tickets.

DOBIE: Tickets?

FRASER: To Ibiza.

JANICE: It's the costume of a desperate man.

DOBIE: Ah. Right. Point taken. See the thing is about your tickets – Davey's got them. So you should maybe wait for him in the basement.

JANICE: We've been waiting.

FRASER: And he's not got them.

DOBIE: Well now then. Leonard must have got them. Do you pair not think I have better things to worry about than dealing with silly wee dolies?

FRASER: Just give me my tickets and give her her rent book back.

JANICE: Fraser! **(To DOBIE)** Tell me what other things you've got to worry about

DOBIE: **(very firmly)** They are beyond your limits! They are outwith your comprehension.

JANICE: Are they matters of life and death?

DOBIE: **(laughing at her)** I meant it, Janice when I said you looked radiant in your nice frock. It would be a shame if you got a horrible big stain on it.

The other lift arrives. They all wait to see who's in it. The doors remain shut.

DOBIE: That'll be Leonard now. **(He faces the lift.)** Leonard. Some pals of yours and I've got another wee job for you. **(The doors remain shut.)** Leonard? **(He takes a step towards the lift and considers.)** Leonard, is that you in there? **(Pause)** Davey? You seen that tube Leonard anywhere? Haha. **(Pause)** Is one of you two floozies stuck in that lift? **(Pause)** Eh?

The lift doors open. The semi-conscious body of ARBOGAST topples into the room. Standing in the lift holding a sawn-off shotgun is a giant of a man in a coat and suit, his clothes covered in burnt patches and smouldering bits; his voice is similarly well-done.

DOBIE: . . . Alec . . .

SNEDDON: Hiya Willie. Heard you were having a party. Fuckin funny I never got an invite. Hiya Janice. Sit down, Willie. I'd've rung you, doll, but some some swine whapped me on the head and drove me away and set my van on fire. My best van with me in the back. You beat that. My best van's a burnt out shell and I never even had the fucker properly insured. **(To DOBIE)** Are you gonnae sit down when I ask you? And see when I woke up and the van was like the inside of a furnace, I think that what happened was that some of my muscles got cooked, you know the muscles in my arms and legs and stuff, so they don't work properly any more. So if you'd sit down when I wave my gun at you, your gun really, Willie, then that'll save me coming over there and havin to try batter you.

DOBIE: I'm sittin down, Alec, look I've sat down.

SNEDDON: Hello, Janice.

JANICE: Hello . . . Alec . . . Alec . . . I didn't . . . I mean I was never aware that . . .

JANICE can't begin to work out what to say to him. In her terror her brain's short-circuiting a bit.

JANICE: Alec . . . Is there anything I can do to make it up to you . . .

SNEDDON smiles.

SNEDDON: Make it up to me? – Janice. Look at me.

FRASER: She's in love with you.

SNEDDON looks at FRASER.

FRASER: That's what she's just after telling me.

SNEDDON: And you believed her did you?

FRASER nods.

FRASER: **(struggles for a micro second, then nods)** Janice is . . . has never faced anything till she faced up to murdering you and then she saw. **(He loses it.)** . . . Janice?

JANICE: I saw . . . you were a good man, Alec. Behind . . . being a bad man. And if I hadn't . . . murdered you . . then maybe

... we could have been happy ...

SNEDDON: **(turning to face DOBIE)** And you weren't wrong there, Willie. A man of taste. Like this place for instance. Nice property, Willie ... Potential.

DOBIE: Aye it needs a lot of cash spent, Alec, but you know, once we all get it tidied up.

SNEDDON: Funny that, cause I got an approach. From Mister Arbogast here. Desiring me to liquidate some assets. You know. My nightclub. Blisters. And I never realised you, William, were the man in charge.

DOBIE: Me? **(DOBIE giggles nervously.)** I'm not the man in ... come on, Alec ... Me? ... Hey ... guys? ...

ARBOGAST moans. Everybody looks at him. He lifts his head and looks at DOBIE. He is badly injured. Concussed and bleeding. He starts dragging himself, interminably and painfully, across the floor towards DOBIE.

SNEDDON: Look at that. Bleedin on the floor then rubbin it in when you're tryin to keep the place tidy. Fuckin despicable. That's David Arbogast Esquire through and through. Do you no think. Willie?

DOBIE: Aye.

SNEDDON: That's certainly my opinion anyway. Still. Poor bastard. That was some wallop I hit him in the car park so maybe you canny really blame him. He's probably got quite serious brain damage he'll never really recover from ... **(Pause. Sneddon looks at ARBOGAST and ponders this.)** ... I reckon. **(He cackles.)** What a hoot **(To JANICE and FRASER)** He's sittin in the car with wee Raymond McFadyen in the front with him, and Raymond's measuring out these pills and Arbogast's sittin next to him fuckin gloatin with a bottle of Johnny Walker's in his hand and he takes a slug and then he stares at the label and I can hear him muttering away under his breath, goin, 'What the fuck's that spotty so and so fuckin spotty balloon gone and purchased . . .' And wee Raymond's goin, '123, 124, 125 . . .' And Davey gets half out the car and holds the bottle up to the light. And I get right behind him and I goes, 'Psst! gies a slug of your juice', and he goes tense and starts to turn his head and I goes BATTER! Hard as I can. BATTER! I gives him another one and he goes, 'For pity's sake, you're killin me friend' in a wee quiet pathetic wee whiney voice and so I goes BATTER – and gives him another one for bein such a hypocrite because if there's one thing I cannot suffer in a fellow human being it's hypocrisy.

FRASER: Did you hurt Raymond?

SNEDDON: Fraser – I couldn't hurt Raymond – great wee guy. Arbogast's all concussed and I says to him, 'What's that you're counting out there Raymond'. He goes, 'Love drugs'. He says, 'They made me make it, I don't even know if I've made it properly'. So I says, 'Why don't we test it out then, on Davey here, cause he looks as though he's in need of a bit of loving', so Raymond crams a handful of his pills down Davey's throat and then I says, 'Okay that's fine Raymond you can just hop it', which he did, though I never meant it that literally, the boy must have been nervous. You love him, Fraser?

FRASER: **(very nervous of SNEDDON)** Love him . . . eh . . . well I don't know if I'd go so far as to. . .

JANICE: Fraser!

FRASER: . . . Yup. I really, really . . . like him.

SNEDDON: Okay. Why don't you pair go and help Raymond with the paraffin, I told him to give us quarter of an hour.

JANICE: Paraffin?

SNEDDON: Aye on you go. And when you're done the three of you can take Willie's car cause he'll no be needin it.

He lobs DOBIE'S car keys to JANICE.

DOBIE: You can borrow my car alright, Janice but I'll have to send Leonard round to get it back.

SNEDDON: **(laughs)** I wouldn't worry about Leonard if I were you, Janice.

DOBIE looks at SNEDDON.

FRASER: **(to SNEDDON)** I was wondering if . . . Just . . . I couldn't put on Leonard's scratchy jumper and he burnt all mine as evidence so I wouldn't get linked . . . after I did the insurance number for him . . . So I just was thinking . . . Can I get his clothes?

SNEDDON gestures to DOBIE.

SNEDDON: Don't be a shy boy, William.

DOBIE undresses and gives FRASER all his clothes. DOBIE stands in his silky black posing pouch. FRASER looks at his own grunties then points at Dobie's.

FRASER: I don't suppose you'd like to swap?

JANICE: Fraser! **(JANICE and FRASER bolt.)**

FRASER and JANICE leave.

DOBIE: You're a bad evil bastard, Alec, and you'll burn in hell.

SNEDDON: Was, Willie, I've reformed. Anyway I've already had a taste of the fiery afterlife courtesy of Willie Dobie

Enterprises. And Raymond told me this marvellous thing once that strengthened me. Do you want to hear it? **(ARBOGAST emits a horrible moan.)** Aye, you as well. Davey, **(To DOBIE)** That'll be the love drug working, the guy's probably dying for his hole. **(To ARBOGAST)** Hoi, you, pay attention and you might learn something, scum. Might emerge a better person. **(To DOBIE)** Do you think he's compos mentos?

DOBIE: **(pleading to be finished)** Will you please just get on with it, Alec.

SNEDDON: Oh. Right. **(His attention comes back to DOBIE. He concentrates.)** See Raymond told me that current thinking is that this universe was created in one huge big explosion that produced loads and loads of . . . stuff. I think it was hydrogen he said. And that's all there was. And it swirled about for . . . Oh . . . hundreds of years until it made stars. And then inside of these stars, Willie, the hydrogen got turned into other stuff. You know by the heat or something. The pressure. And I can appreciate that. I'm not a hundred per cent sure but anyway. It made gold and lead and iron and uranium and all the expensive precious stuff. And that's what makes us. All these chemicals inside us that make us work came from the inside of a star. Is that not an exceptional piece of knowledge. Willie. **(Pause)** You agree with me. That you and me and David Arbogast and everybody else, no matter what they're like as a person, is made out of stardust. I found that exceptionally moving. **(ARBOGAST has reached the side of DOBIE'S chair.)**

DOBIE: What is it you're saying, Sneddon?

SNEDDON: **(angry)** Nothing. I'm saying! . . . I'm just saying isn't it delightful the way we've all got something to teach one another!

DOBIE: Yes, but what is it that you're saying to me?

SNEDDON: I'm not 'saying' anything! I'm telling you something, Willie!

DOBIE: Okay, okay. All I'm saying is I don't understand what it is you're telling me. Am I supposed to find that . . .

SNEDDON: You're not supposed to find it anything, it's just a personal story to . . . so that . . . **(He gestures at ARBOGAST, shouting at DOBIE.)** Don't just let the poor guy crawl around on his hands and knees all night, get up off your arse and let him sit down.

ARBOGAST has slumped with the effort of crawling across the floor towards DOBIE, he is only semi-conscious, he dribbles and mumbles very quietly.

SNEDDON: Willie, give him a help up for God's sake, can you no see he's injured.

DOBIE hauls at ARBOGAST. Eyes fixed on SNEDDON.

SNEDDON: That's the way, show him a bit of care and compassion and make him comfy.

DOBIE gets ARBOGAST onto the seat. ARBOGAST'S head lolls.

ARBOGAST: **(almost inaudibly)** I told you Willie. I'm going to . . . **(His voice fades away altogether.)**

SNEDDON: What did he say?

DOBIE: I don't know, I can't hear him.

SNEDDON: Lean down and listen then, you ill-mannered get!

DOBIE leans down and puts his ear next to ARBOGAST'S mouth. ARBOGAST tries to speak again.

SNEDDON: What did he say?

DOBIE: **(shouts)** I can't hear him!

SNEDDON: Well concentrate. Try! The pair of you. Davey speak up for God's sake. **(ARBOGAST tries again.)** Eh?

DOBIE bends down and listens some more.

DOBIE: He says 'I told you, Willie.'

SNEDDON: Told you what?

DOBIE leans down again. ARBOGAST grabs DOBIE and hauls his head down. He repeats himself. DOBIE breaks free. He straightens up and faces SNEDDON.

DOBIE: He says 'I told you, Willie, I am going to rip out your spinal column.'

SNEDDON: **(laughs)** Good on you, Davey. Well said, son.

DOBIE: What do you want, Alec. I can only say I'm very sorry.

SNEDDON: What do I want. Look at me. Well. I can only say I'm happy you're sorry. I want to see what you're really made of, Bill.

DOBIE: Uhuh.

SNEDDON: I want you to do a favour for me.

DOBIE: What?

SNEDDON: Then I'm willing to not shoot you.

DOBIE: What is it.

SNEDDON: But if you don't do my favour for me – I shoot you.

DOBIE: Tell me the favour.

SNEDDON: **(pause)** Strangle him.

DOBIE: **(pause)** Why?

SNEDDON: Because I want you to find out if you can do it.

DOBIE: I don't understand, I don't want to strangle him.

SNEDDON: If you don't understand, then I have to shoot you. I will, you know. I'll shoot off your legs and leave you here to burn.

DOBIE: No, don't shoot me Alec, but I don't see why . . .

SNEDDON pumps the gun and aims at DOBIE. DOBIE stares back and places his hands on ARBOGAST'S throat.

SNEDDON: Show me you can do it, William. Use your thumbs.

DOBIE strangles ARBOGAST. ARBOGAST tries to laugh. SNEDDON watches. ARBOGAST dies.

SNEDDON: Is that him murdered? **(DOBIE nods.)** Off you go then, Willie.

DOBIE: Eh? **(He unclamps his fingers from ARBOGAST'S throat.)**

SNEDDON: Skedaddle. Leave me in peace.

DOBIE backs towards the lift. He opens the door. Smoke billows out.

SNEDDON: Oops. Raymond's a bit fuckin punctual with the paraffin. Looks like you stay here with me and Davey and burn. **(DOBIE turns.)**

DOBIE: In your dreams, Alec.

He hits the alarm bell and gets into the lift, he slams the doors shut and starts banging and calling and coughing. Smoke pours out the gaps and cracks. The lift glows with a fiery light.

SNEDDON: And believe you me, it's a whole lot worse than you can begin to imagine.

We hear DOBIE'S voice above the roar of the gathering inferno.

DOBIE: Hey! Girls. Hey! Call the lift. Hey! Press the button and call the lift up! Hey! Princess! Call the . . . Hey! Petal! Pumpkin! Darlin! Would you press the button and please . . . please. Call the lift up and get me out of here. Holly!

DOBIE dies. Nat King Cole sings 'Stardust'. A mirror ball descends from the ceiling and sparkly starbursts fill the room. SNEDDON listens to the first verse then raises the shotgun to his face, wraps his mouth round the barrel and looks up at the mirror ball. The sound of the insectocutor amplified and blackout.

End

The Waltzer

Rhiannon Tise

The Waltzer is a touching and sensitive exploration of the serious business of growing up. A world of beleaguered single parents and adolescent fears and friendships is reflected in the dark mirror of Sally's experience on her first real date. The garish glamour and hectic motion of the fairground and the Waltzer itself provide a perfect setting for this multi-faceted depiction of the thrills and spills of a teenager's first steps towards the adult world. Written for radio, The Waltzer draws much of its power and point from the complex interaction between past and present events, inner monologue and intercut dialogue. In our film and TV dominated culture we can easily miss out on the imaginative strength of radio drama – the publication of this play is a timely reminder of the real alternatives to the siren call of MTV, Cartoon Network and the Disney Channel.

Hugh Hodgart, Head of Acting at RSAMD, Glasgow

ISBN 0-9545206-3-7

£5.99

Available from Booksource Tel: 0870 240 2182
and www.capercailliebooks.co.uk

King Matt

Stephen Greenhorn

King Matt, the story of a boy who becomes a king, is a simple fable filled with surprisingly complex resonances. In common with the very best in storytelling for children, it confronts the big moral issues surrounding the way in which one makes one's way in the world and through life: self-interest vying with self-sacrifice, the greed of the individual with the needs of the collective. The boy-king Matt is undoubtedly the hero of the tale but it is his human faults and frailties as well as his intrepid spirit that keep us on the edge of our seats right up to the suspense-filled ending. This is a play written for children that children would have great fun playing for themselves.

Hugh Hodgart, Head of Acting at RSAMD, Glasgow

A highly articulate play that speaks volumes about the nature of democracy and personal responisibility.

The Stage

ISBN 0-9545206-2-9

£5.99

Available from Booksource Tel: 0870 240 2182
and www.capercailliebooks.co.uk

Dr Korczak's Example

David Greig

Dr Korczak's Example is set in the final, numbered, days of an orphanage in the Warsaw ghetto in 1942. Based on real events, this 'Brechtian' retelling generates an almost unbearable power and pathos through the simple humanity, warts and all, of the central characters who are trapped both by the inexorable forces of Nazi oppression and by our fore-knowledge of the fate that awaits them. The play's 'alienation' device of depicting its characters through the use of dolls, further enhances our painful feeling of powerlessness. Yet, in spite of its tragic outcome, Dr Korczak's Example, like the real life of its protagonist, leaves us exhilarated and uplifted by the indomitable power of love.

Hugh Hodgart, Head of Acting at RSAMD, Glasgow

This is the dramatist's art turned to serve an idea of theatre which is unreproducable in any other medium – a play not to forget.

Will Hutton, The Observer

ISBN 0-9545206-1-0

£5.99

Available from Booksource Tel: 0870 240 2182
and www.capercailliebooks.co.uk

Kaahini

Maya Chowdhry

Kaahini is a highly original yet thoroughly accessible insight into what it means to be young, Asian and British. Filled with the powerful and contradictory emotions of adolescence, Kaahini is brightly coloured, full of warmth and feeling, and shot through with the darker threads of frustration and anger at the inflexible and inexplicable adult world. This play, for all its seemingly unfamiliar Asian context, speaks directly to the widest possible audience: anyone with a mother, father, son, daughter, friend or lover will find much to challenge and inspire them here.

Hugh Hodgart, Head of Acting at RSAMD, Glasgow

Maya Chowdhry's Kaahini is a surprising, tender and beautifully observed play, which manages the elusive feat of exploring gender and cultural politics in a thought-provoking way without ever distracting from the passionate heart of its story. A play which deserves to be seen by as many young people as possible.

John E McGrath, Artistic Director, Contact, Manchester

ISBN 0-9545206-4-5

£5.99

Available from Booksource Tel: 0870 240 2182
and www.capercailliebooks.co.uk

Sunburst Finish

Andrea Gibb
Paddy Cunneen

'Note to self. You are dying.' As a young man's depression turns to despair, suicide seems the only way out - the only way to take control. In spite of the bleakness of its subject, *Sunburst Finish* is filled with strong and vibrant voices, a rich mosaic of music, wit, warmth, insight, feeling, and a remarkable lack of sentimentality. The central character's struggle to come to terms with himself and the world around him is one that all young (and not so young) people will relate strongly to.

Hugh Hodgart, Head of Acting at RSAMD, Glasgow

ISBN 0-9545206-5-3

£5.99

Available from Booksource Tel: 0870 240 2182
and www.capercailliebooks.co.uk

Shakespeare The Director's Cut

Michael Bogdanov

This collection of cutting-edge essays is a valuable addition to Shakespeare studies, and to theatre studies more generally. Michael Bogdanov's cuts are always incisive, razor-sharp, and applied with an unerring hand. Never dogmatic or programmatic, Bogdanov approaches each play attentive to its novelty and its nuances, alive to its urgency and impact, attuned to its language and its lore. As a director acutely aware of critical conventions – enough to want to overturn them – Bogdanov is uniquely positioned to combine theoretical acuity with a practitioner's knowledge of what works on the page and in performance, while never losing sight of what is most politically resonant and socially engaged. The meat is moist closest to the bone, and these are choice cuts from a master butcher.

Willy Maley, Professor of Renaissance Studies,
University of Glasgow

For 30 years Michael Bogdanov has been the most consistently interesting and provocative of British directors of Shakespeare. Now he has written a series of incisive essays on the plays – not comments on his many productions, but introductions to the works that show the result of his long acquaintance with them. The essays, based in social thought and theatrical savvy, make Shakespeare accessible and immediate and will be of interest to a wide range of readers.

Dennis Kennedy, Beckett Professor of Drama,
Trinity College Dublin

Michael Bogdanov is the Tyrone Guthrie of our day, and his signature is all over the work of many young directors. He is at once scholar, provocateur, puritan and Lord of Misrule.

Michael Pennington

ISBN 0-9545206-0-2

£8.99

Available from Booksource Tel: 0870 240 2182
and www.capercailliebooks.co.uk
From all major bookshops and www.amazon.co.uk